Thinking
About Program
Evaluation

Thinking About Program Evaluation

Richard A. Berk
Peter H. Rossi

SAGE PUBLICATIONS
The International Professional Publishers
Newbury Park   London   New Delhi

Copyright © 1990 by Sage Publications, Inc.

For information address:

SAGE Publications, Inc.
2455 Teller Road
Newbury Park, California 91320

SAGE Publications Ltd.
6 Bonhill Street
London EC2A 4PU
United Kingdom

SAGE Publications India Pvt. Ltd.
M-32 Market
Greater Kailash I
New Delhi 110 048 India

H
62
.B428
1990
Dept.
Oct. 2009

$32.00

Printed in the United States of America

Library of Congress Cataloging-in-Publication Data

Berk, Richard A.
    Thinking about program evaluation / Richard A. Berk, Peter H. Rossi.
        p.   cm.
    ISBN 0-8039-3704-0. -- ISBN 0-8039-3705-9 (pbk.)
        1. Evaluation research (Social action programs)--Utilization.
    I. Rossi, Peter Henry, 1921- .   II. Title.
    H62.B428   1990
    361.6'068'4--dc20   89-28655
                                                               CIP

91 92 93 94 15 14 13 12 11 10 9 8 7 6 5 4 3

Contents

1. What This Book Is About 7
2. Key Concepts in Evaluation Research 12
3. Designing New Programs: A Chronological
   Perspective 33
4. Examining Ongoing Programs: A Chronological
   Perspective 63
   Some Final Observations 98
   Appendix: Guide to Literature on, Professional
   Associations of, and Organizations Engaged in
   Evaluation Research and Social Policy Research
   in the United States 101

References 119
Index 125
About the Authors 127

1

What This Book Is About

Program evaluation derives from the commonsense idea that social programs should have demonstrable benefits. Literacy programs for adults, for example, should lead to measurable improvements in reading skill. Lowering speed limits on interstate highways should plainly reduce the number of automobile fatalities and save gasoline. Increasing the length of prison sentences for white-collar crime should clearly reduce the amount of insider trading. Increasing the price of electricity during the middle of the day should visibly reduce consumption during "peak load" hours. Efforts to educate sexually active individuals about "safe sex" should plainly slow the spread of AIDS. Implicit is the notion that social programs ought to have explicit aims by which success or failure may be empirically judged. Mere assertions about success or failure are insufficient. The assertions must be supported by evidence.

It should not be surprising, therefore, that program evaluation, broadly construed, has a long history. In ancient Rome, for instance, tax policies were altered in response to observed fluctuations in revenues. During the last decades of the eighteenth century, the British Admiralty began requiring that its crews drink citrus juice on long voyages after evidence was produced showing that citrus juice prevented scurvy. Early in the twentieth century, the indeterminate prison sentence was introduced in the United States, partly in response to the high rates of recidivism under earlier sentencing policies. In short, judgments have always been made about whether prospective or ongoing programs are effective.

In recent years, however, commonsense program evaluation has evolved into "evaluation *research*," a heterogeneous mix of substantive issues and procedures of considerable sophistication and power. Evaluation research includes the design of social programs, the ongoing monitoring of how well programs are functioning, the assessment of program impact, and the analysis of the program benefits relative to their costs. One might inquire, for example, whether a job training program is reaching the people most in need of help (i.e., a monitoring question) and then whether the training demonstrably leads to greater success in the labor market (i.e., an impact question).

Moreover, a range of research methods are employed: ethnography, survey research, randomized experiments, benefit-cost analysis, and others. A wide range of methods is used because different methods have different strengths and weaknesses, and because the particular questions being asked should be coupled with the most effective research methods. For example, in designing a program, it is always important to know what the target population is. The size and nature of the target population (e.g., unemployed teenagers) typically is best determined by survey procedures.

Finally, evaluation research capitalizes on existing theory and empirical generalizations from the social sciences. Understanding of why a particular water or energy conservation plan failed (or succeeded), for instance, might be greatly enhanced by insights from both microeconomics and social psychology. Likewise, a lot might be learned from sociology and psychology about how to devise programs to reduce teenage pregnancy.

Yet, such advances would be irrelevant without the interest and support of policymakers and other interested parties who believe that social programs should be empirically accountable and that evaluation research has something to offer. That is, without interest *and* funding from organizations or agencies who have a stake in whether a particular program is working, evaluation research would soon wither away. At its best, however, evaluation research can only help policymakers make judgments about the relative success or failure of programs and policies, whether these be prospective or in operation. Evaluation research is *not* a substitute for policymaker judgments, and responsible evaluators have no interest in either circumventing the political process or becoming central players.

Put another way, evaluation research is essentially about the provision of the most accurate information practically possible in an evenhanded manner. For example, an evaluation study might determine the likely impact of a program providing information about sexually transmitted diseases to adolescent schoolchildren but leave unaddressed the political question of whether the schools should make such programs mandatory. Similarly, an evaluation might estimate the degree to which charges for the treatment of waste water would deter manufacturers from polluting but be silent on the fairness of such pricing policies. Or an evaluation might determine that bottle-ban initiatives really reduce litter but take no position on whether such bans are an unreasonable interference with a free market.

So, what then is a *successful* evaluation? To anticipate a bit, an evaluation attains *practical* perfection when it provides the best information possible on the key policy questions within the given set of real-world constraints. This implies that *all* evaluations are flawed if measured against the yardstick of *abstract* perfection or if judged without taking time, budget, ethical, and political restrictions into account. In other words, there is really no such thing as a truly perfect evaluation, and idealized textbook treatments of research design and analysis typically establish useful aspirations but unrealistic expectations.

A "merely" successful evaluation, in contrast, falls short of providing the best information possible under the given circumstances but provides better information than would otherwise have been available. That is, the proper measure of "success" is current knowledge, not what ultimately might be good to know. Thus, if very little is known about the effectiveness of a particular program, a relatively weak evaluation on a pure methodological scale may nevertheless be an enormous success in practice. For example, if virtually nothing is known about whether perpetrators of family violence can be deterred by an arrest, a single (flawed) evaluation may be extremely successful (Sherman and Cohn 1989).

Note that nothing is being said about how the evaluation is ultimately used. Indeed, an evaluation may be successful even if the information provided is ignored, or even misused. Once the findings are presented in a clear and accessible fashion, the evaluation is over. What follows is certainly critical, but is essentially a political process. Interested evaluators are best off observing the action at some distance, preferably through heavy lenses.

Goals and Organization of This Book

This book provides an introduction to the variety of purposes for which evaluation research may be used and to the range of methods that are currently employed. Specific examples are given to provide concrete illustrations of both the goals of evaluation researchers and the methods used. Although the book is intended to be comprehensive in the sense of describing major uses of evaluation research, it cannot pretend to be encyclopedic. Citations to more detailed discussions are provided. In addition, there are several general references that survey the field of evaluation in a more detailed fashion (Suchman 1967; Weiss 1972; Cronbach and Associates 1980; Rossi and Freeman 1989; Cronbach 1982; Guba and Lincoln 1981; Guttentag and Struening 1975; Cook and Campbell 1979).

The book is consciously designed to address central ideas within two formats. First, *key concepts* are briefly introduced, in part as a kind of dictionary for later discussions. The goal is to acquaint the reader with a few fundamental ideas. Second, the evaluation research enterprise is presented in an idealized, *chronological* fashion to emphasize that the research methods employed depend on the empirical question being asked and the evolution of the social program under scrutiny. For example, research procedures that might well make sense as a program is initially being designed may be ineffective when the impact of an ongoing program is being addressed. Likewise, research procedures that are effective in determining *how* a program works will often differ from research procedures that are effective in determining *whether* a program works. In short, our message is pragmatic; research tools should be chosen for the particular job at hand.

2

Key Concepts in
Evaluation Research

We turn initially to a number of central concepts in evaluation research. Because the main intellectual roots of evaluation research are found in the social sciences, social science concepts and research methods predominate. All social science fields have contributed to the development of evaluation research methods. It is not surprising, therefore, that the best evaluation research and the best evaluators draw on a number of disciplines, using an eclectic repertoire of concepts and methods.

As we proceed, below, we will begin with the policy environment in which evaluation research is undertaken, because policy questions provide motivation for the entire evaluation research enterprise. Then, we move on to technical matters. However, the boundaries between policy concerns and technical concerns are often unclear, in part because both have implications for one another. From the start, we stress that evaluation research is not a laboratory science.

Policy Space

The substantive roots of evaluation research rest in policy concerns, and evaluations are almost entirely confined to issues that are contained in the current "policy space." That is, evaluations are almost exclusively concerned with making judgments about policies and programs that are on the current agenda of policymakers (broadly construed to include a wide variety of "players," not just public officials). Clearly, the policy space is time and space bound and does not encompass a permanently fixed set of policies and programs; it changes over time and it varies over political jurisdictions. For example, in the 1960s, the national policy space in the United States included direct income support, in the form of a "negative income tax," for households falling below the poverty line. In response, a number of evaluation projects explored what the impact of such support might be. In the 1980s, the national policy space no longer includes a negative income tax. Likewise, in the middle 1970s communities across the State of California were considering a wide variety of water conservation programs because of a serious drought. By the early 1980s, other problems dominated the local policy space, in part because the drought had passed.

It is the almost exclusive attention to matters in current policy space that distinguishes evaluation research from academic social science, and a good evaluation researcher knows how to determine what is in the policy space and what is not. For example, an academic social scientist might study the "urban underclass" as an intellectual matter and may in addition be genuinely concerned about their plight. In contrast, the evaluation researcher would focus on the current policy debates and especially social interventions that are being contemplated or are already in place. Still more concretely, the academic might have a long-standing interest in theories of segmented labor markets and undertake a study of the causes of teenage unemployment to test competing theories. The evaluator could certainly draw on insights from such research but might concentrate, for instance, on the impact of a particular job training program for unemployed teenagers.

Stakeholders

By virtue of its engagement in policy space matters, evaluation research is saturated with political concerns. The outcome of an evaluation can be expected to attract the attention of persons, groups, and agencies who hold stakes in the outcome. These "stakeholders" include policymakers on the executive and legislative levels; the agencies and their officials who administer the policies or programs under scrutiny; the persons who deliver the services in question; often, groups representing the targets or beneficiaries of the programs, or the targets or beneficiaries themselves; and sometimes taxpayers and citizens generally. In almost all program issues, stakeholders may be aligned on opposing sides, some favoring the program and some opposing. And whatever the outcome of the evaluation may be, there are usually some who are pleased and some who are disappointed: It is usually impossible to please everyone. For example, an evaluation showing the benefits of allowing convicts to be employed by private firms (e.g., to manufacture furniture) might be strongly endorsed by prisoners' rights groups, prison officials, and local chambers of commerce but be roundly criticized by law enforcement groups, law-and-order legislators, and labor unions.

In short, an evaluation report ordinarily is not regarded as a neutral document: Rather, it is scrutinized, often minutely, by stakeholders who are quick to discern how its contents affect their activities. Even when an evaluation is conducted "in house"—by an agency concerned with its own activities— stakeholders may appear within the agency to appraise the report's implications.[1] One implication is that evaluation research should not to be undertaken by persons who prefer to avoid controversy, or who have difficulty facing criticism. Often, moreover, the criticism is "political" and not motivated by scientific concerns. A second implication is that much greater care may need to be taken in the conduct of evaluation research than in the conduct of its academic cousin, basic research. Procedures bordering on the slipshod will surely come to the attention of critical stakeholders and render an evaluation report vulnerable. In addition, even for well-conducted studies, attacks will typically focus on "methodological issues" because, as noted earlier, *all* studies have methodological flaws (more on that shortly). Alleged methodological errors are easy targets.[2] A third implication is that the conduct of evaluation research often involves careful prior negotiations with stakeholders. An evaluation of a within-school educational program will be seriously impeded, for example, if a teachers' organization recommends that its members not cooperate with the evaluator.

Program Effectiveness: Three Meanings

While the importance of the political environment in which evaluation research is undertaken is hard to overemphasize, political matters are hardly the whole story. A mixed bag of legitimate technical skills are the evaluator's ticket of admission and in the end justify his or her keep. We turn, then, to technical matters, beginning with conceptions of the proverbial bottom line: program effectiveness.

In the broadest sense, evaluations are concerned with whether or not programs or policies are achieving their goals and purposes. Discerning the goals of policies and programs is an essential part of an evaluation and almost always its starting point. However, goals and purposes are often stated vaguely, typically in an attempt to garner as much political support as possible. Programs and policies that do not have clear and consistent goals cannot be evaluated for their effectiveness. In response, a subspecialty of evaluation research, evaluability assessment, has developed to uncover the goals and purposes of policies and programs in order to judge whether or not they can be evaluated.

Insofar as goals are articulated, "effectiveness" is the extent to which a policy or program is achieving its goals and purposes. In practice, it cannot be overemphasized that the concept of effectiveness must always address the issue: "compared with what?" For *marginal* effectiveness the issue is dosage; the consequences of more or less of some intervention are assessed. For example, one might study whether decreasing by one-half the ratio of grade school students to their teachers later doubles student performance on standardized reading tests. For *relative* effectiveness, the contrast is between a program and the absence of the program or between two or more program options.[3] For example, one might compare the impact on the number of cancer screenings generated by public service announcements versus the number generated by mass mailings of pamphlets, both containing the same educational information. Finally, it is common to consider effectiveness in dollar terms: *cost-effectiveness*. Comparisons are made in units of outcome per dollar. For example, vaccinating the elderly for influenza would probably be less effective in reducing the number of flu-related fatalities for all age groups than vaccinating everyone regardless of age. However, focusing on the elderly may be more cost-effective because, with mass vaccinations, a large number of people would be vaccinated who were not significantly at risk. That is, the cost per life saved would be lower.

Validity

It is one thing to properly conceptualize program effectiveness and quite another to determine empirically whether a program is effective. And determining effectiveness depends, in turn, on the validity of the evaluation. In other words, evaluation research shares with other research activities the overriding goal of achieving high validity. Little is learned from evaluations with low validity.

Broadly stated, validity represents a set of scientific criteria by which the *credibility* of research may be judged. As such, it involves matters of degree; studies are more or less valid. For example, there is currently a heated controversy about the degree to which findings from studies using mice to determine the carcinogenic impact of various environmental pollutants may be properly applied to humans (Freedman and Zeisel 1988). We stress, in addition, that views of evaluators may differ on which kinds of validity are most important (e.g., Cronbach 1982), and what validity means may change over time as methodological technology evolves. Nevertheless, it is common to emphasize four kinds of validity: construct validity, internal validity, external validity, and statistical conclusion validity (Cook and Campbell, 1979). We will return to the four kinds of validity after laying a bit more groundwork.

Ideally, policymakers are seeking a binary assessment about a social program: thumbs up or thumbs down. Either the program works or it does not. In addition, they are ideally seeking a specific number indicating how effective the program is. Thus a prison vocational training program might reduce recidivism by 15%. Or a nutrition program for pregnant women in low-income neighborhoods may increase the birth weight of infants by an average 2.3 pounds. Or a company's affirmative action program may increase by 15 the number of Blacks and Latinos hired. As just noted, however, the world of program evaluation is never that simple. *All* assessments come with healthy amounts of uncertainty, and evaluation results necessarily have varying amounts of credibility. To be sure, studies with greater validity provide more credible results, but some uncertainty will always remain. That is, evaluation findings are not right or wrong, but more or less credible. Typically, the uncertainty is expressed in how the role of chance is represented but that is hardly the whole story (see below).

It is perhaps important to stress, as well, that the uncertainty in evaluation results is inherent in the social phenomena being studied and no research methodology, even the ideal, can remove it. However, stronger research methods typically reduce the amount of uncertainty.

Measurement and Construct Validity

Measurement is nothing more than a systematic procedure to assign (real) numbers to objects. "Age," for example, may be measured by the number of years between birth and the present. "Prior record" may be measured by a "1" if there is a previous conviction and a "0" if there is no previous conviction. "Attitudes toward water conservation" may be measured by a "3," "2," or "1" depending, respectively, on whether a person answers "agree," "uncertain," or "disagree" to a survey question on the importance of installing water-saving appliances.

Better measures lead to better evaluations (other things being equal). A "good" measure is, in commonsense terms, one that is likely to measure accurately what it is supposed to measure. For example, a study estimating the impact of the Centers for Disease Control's pamphlet on AIDS, recently mailed to all U.S. households, must use measures that properly capture what CDC intended to affect in the way of behavioral, attitudinal, and cognitive change. This would be no small task. Questions about measurement quality would apply not only to program outcomes such as "safe sex," but also to measures of the program itself and to other factors that may be at work. For example, a measure of the intervention may be whether individuals read the pamphlet; a factor affecting safe sex may be regular reading of major newsmagazines. Measurement in evaluation research is sometimes discussed under the rubric of *construct validity* (Cook and Campbell 1979).

At a minimum, evaluation researchers should be aware of the critical distinction between two kinds of measurement error: *systematic* and *random*. When the measurement error is systematic, there will be on the average an overestimate or underestimate of the "true" attribute that is being measured. This is at the heart of the perennial controversy over whether standardized IQ tests really tap "general intelligence" in a culture-free manner. Some argue that Blacks, on the average, score less than Whites because Black intelligence is systematically underestimated by the commonly used tests. When the measurement error is random (or "noise"), the measures, on the average, will equal the true attribute, but will be inaccurate to varying degrees for individual instances. That is, the measured IQ for each person will be a flawed measure of intelligence, but if the IQ test could be given a large number of times to each person (with no learning effects), the average of each person's IQ scores would be equal to each person's true intelligence.

It should be clear that systematic measurement error can seriously distort one's evaluation findings. It is also true, however, that random measurement error can be very damaging. When the random measurement error is in the outcome variable(s) of interest, "noise" can obscure real treatment effects. That is, real results may be overlooked. When the random measurement error is in the treatment (e.g., who got which intervention) or the control variables (i.e., variables whose effects need to be disentangled from the effects of the treatment), estimates of the treatment effect can be systematically too high or too low. That is, estimates of treatment impact will be *biased*. Whether approached as an "errors in variables" problem as in the econometric literature (e.g., Kmenta 1971; 309–22), as a "latent variable" problem as in the psychometric literature (Lord 1980), or as the "underadjustment" problem in the evaluation literature (e.g., Campbell and Erlebacher 1970), random error can lead to decidedly nonrandom distortions in evaluation results. The role of random measurement error is sometimes addressed through the concept of "reliability."

Causality and Internal Validity

Many evaluation questions concern causal relations, such as whether or not a proposed program encouraging people not to use wood-burning stoves on high air pollution days will "cause" reductions in air pollution. The literature on causality and causal inference is large and, currently, fraught with controversy (e.g., Pratt and Schlaifer 1984; Holland 1986; Holland and Rubin 1988; Berk 1988b). Suffice it to say that by a "causal effect" we mean a comparison between the outcome had the intervention been introduced compared to the outcome had the intervention not been introduced. For example, the causal effect of a ban on diesel-powered automobiles might be the amount of nitrogen-based pollutants in the air had diesel automobile engines been banned compared to the amount had the ban not been put in place.

From the definition of a causal effect, it should be apparent that, in practice, causal effects cannot be directly observed. One cannot observe the amount of nitrogen-based pollutants in the air simultaneously with and without the ban on diesel engines in place. Rather, causal effects must be inferred. Thus one might try to estimate the causal effect of the ban by comparing air quality before the ban to air quality after. Or one might try to estimate the causal effect of the ban by comparing air quality in an area with the ban to air quality in an area without the ban. In the first case, however, one must assume that no other changes had occurred that could affect air quality in the interval between the earlier and later observational periods. In the second case, one must assume that the two areas are otherwise effectively identical on all factors that could influence air quality. In short, the need to infer causal effects opens the door to inferential errors.

In practice, therefore, whenever a causal relationship is proposed, alternative explanations must be addressed and, presumably, discarded. If such alternatives are not considered, one may be led to make "spurious" causal inferences; the causal relationship being proposed may not in fact exist. Sometimes this concern with spurious causation is addressed under the heading of *internal validity* (Cook and Campbell 1979). For example, anyone who claims that an educational TV program improved the knowledge of those who viewed it must also consider the alternative explanation that viewers were self-selected persons interested in the topic who would have acquired the same amount of information in some other way were the program not available.

The consideration of alternative causal explanations for the success of programs is an extremely important consideration when plans to collect the data are formulated (Heckman and Robb 1985). In the wood-burning example, an observed change in air pollution after the program went into effect may have been caused by milder weather, improved wood-burning equipment, or a rise in cord wood prices leading people to shift to other fuels. The social intervention could be totally irrelevant.

In addition, programs that deal with humans are all more or less subject to problems of self-selection; often persons who are most likely to be helped, or who are already on the road to recovery, are those most likely to participate in a program.

Thus vocational training offered to unemployed adults is likely to attract those who would be most apt to improve their employment situation in any event. Or, sometimes, program operators "skim off the cream" among target populations for participation in programs, thereby assuring that such programs appear successful. In still other cases, events unconnected with the program produce changes that seem to result from the program being evaluated: An improvement in the speed with which cases are processed by a county's courts may seem to result from the addition of more prosecutors to the local district attorney's office, when actually, the improvement may have been caused by an unconnected change in plea-bargaining practices. In any case, we will have more to say about causal inference later.

Generalizability and External Validity

Whatever the empirical conclusions resulting from evaluation research, it is necessary to consider how broadly one can generalize the findings in question; that is, are the findings relevant to other times, other subjects, similar programs, and other program sites? Sometimes such concerns are raised under the rubric of *external validity* (Cook and Campbell 1979).

It cannot be overemphasized that, if findings cannot be generalized, they are useless. Policymakers need to know how interventions of certain *kinds* work and if those *kinds* of interventions are effective. Knowing how a particular program worked and how effective it was by itself has no value, because that program can never be exactly duplicated. The best that policymakers can do is mount a program that is (more or less) *similar* to the program evaluated.

Consider, for instance, a program to reduce the consumption of electricity during the middle of the day (the "peak load" problem) by raising the price of electricity between 10:00 in the morning and 4:00 in the afternoon. Suppose the evaluation convincingly showed that raising the price by 15% led to a drop of 10% in electricity use during the peak load hours. However, the economic environment in which the intervention was introduced is constantly changing, and this will affect not only the base price of electricity on which the 15% increase may be calculated but the fraction of each consumer's budget that is allocated to the purchase of electricity. For example, if the base price of electricity is low relative to the price of gas, consumers may purchase electric stoves rather than gas stoves and electric dryers rather than gas dryers. New homes may be built with electric heat rather than gas heat. Over the medium term, therefore, the consumption of electricity may *increase*. Moreover, consumer concern about energy shortages will depend on a variety of varying factors, such as the way in which OPEC is depicted in American mass media. In short, it is far from obvious what use policymakers could make of the evaluation unless one grants some license to generalize.

The key, therefore, is being able to make statements about energy conservation programs *like* the one evaluated. If the study is well designed (more on that later) and if good social science theory exists on how consumers respond to price, policymakers may confidently conclude that, *in general*, peaktime price increases will reduce energy use during the middle of the day and that the response of consumers to increases in the price of electricity will be much like the responses estimated. For example, micro-economic theory may confirm that increases in the marginal (per unit) price will reduce consumption almost regardless of circumstances and that the "price elasticity" for particular commodities will be effectively constant across different times, places, and mixes of residential consumers. In other words, while the electricity conservation program evaluated is literally unique, it may well be possible to draw more general conclusions. *External validity*, then, refers to the degree to which these kinds of generalizations are justified.

More broadly, among the standard external validity concerns that can be raised about most evaluations is whether the findings are applicable to *settings* differing from the ones in which the evaluation was undertaken. "Settings" can include a country, state, county, city, neighborhood, school district, business firm, hospital, and so on. For example, "safe houses" for wife battery victims may only be effective in urban areas where the location of the safe house can far more easily be kept secret. Likewise, an affirmative action program that might be effective in virtually all private universities might fail at public universities.

It is also common to wonder whether an evaluation's results would be applicable to *persons* who differ from the study's participants in abilities or in socioeconomic background. For example, *Sesame Street* was found to be effective for preschool children from lower socioeconomic families but more effective for children from middle-class families (Cook et al. 1975). In contrast, arresting men who assault their wives seems to deter many future assaults regardless of the assailant's age, education, or race (Berk and Sherman 1988). The same issues arise, incidentally, for all kinds of experimental units such as households, police departments, and prisons.

There is also the problem of generalizing over *time.* For example, Maynard and Murnane (1979) found that transfer payments provided by the Gary Income Maintenance Experiment apparently increased the reading scores of children from the experimental families. One possible explanation is that, with income subsidies, parents (especially in single-parent families) were able to work less and, therefore, spend more time with their children. Even if this were true, it raises the question of whether similar effects would be found at present, when inflation is taking a smaller bite out of the purchasing power of households.

Finally, there is the difficulty of generalizing over *interventions,* because no two treatments are likely to be identical. Consider, for instance, the content of a literacy program for adults. There are a wide variety of ways literacy may be taught and, within these forms, a wide variety of teaching styles, classroom arrangements, incentive systems, and teaching materials. Even with clear and lengthy guidelines, full standardization is impossible. Thus literacy programs integrated into more general vocational training may well have different results from literacy programs taught on a stand-alone basis: One cannot generalize from one approach to another.

Another way of thinking about generalization is to recognize that programs vary in their *"robustness"*; that is, in their ability to produce the same results with different operators, different clientele, in different settings, and at different historical times. Clearly, a "robust" program is highly desirable. For example, many medical interventions, such as vaccination programs for influenza, are relatively robust because, for purposes of fighting disease, medical treatments can often be effectively standardized and humans tend to respond in a sufficiently homogeneous manner.

It should be clear that external validity is a vital issue in all evaluations, which may be handled well or poorly. Basically, there are three devices that evaluators can employ to improve external validity. First, an *unbiased sample* of a defined population (e.g., via a probability sample) justifies generalization back to that population. Thus findings from a random sample of students from a given high school may be generalized to all students in that school. However, the sampling procedures do *not* by themselves justify generalizations to students in other high schools, even in the same school district.

Second, *replications* of a given evaluation may be used to incrementally define the boundaries within which generalization is possible. By "replications," we mean new studies that are as similar as possible to the original study for which generalization was problematic. Note that it is the study that is being replicated; the original findings may or may not be replicated. For example, an experiment in Minneapolis showing that arresting wife batterers reduced their subsequent violent behavior is currently being replicated in six different cities (Berk and Sherman 1988). The goal, in part, is to determine the range of settings in which arresting wife batterers is truly a deterrent. The "content" of an arrest, for instance, can vary by jurisdiction with arrests in some areas including a day or more in jail (awaiting a bail hearing) and arrests in other areas leading to almost immediate release after booking.

Finally, existing *theory* or *empirical generalizations* may be used for generalizing evaluation findings. For example, micro-economic theory asserts that virtually all consumers will respond to price increases by buying less of the particular commodity. Hence, an evaluation in a single community showing that increasing the price of water leads to reduced residential water use may be widely generalized (Berk et al. 1981). Unfortunately, it is very rare in the social sciences to find theory that both is widely accepted and leads to broad generalizations.

Chance and Construct Validity

The nature of chance in social phenomena has a long and controversial history, but for present purposes, chance plays a role whenever uncertainty exists. Basically, there are three (probably complementary) perspectives. First, uncertainty may result from how the data were collected. Second, uncertainty may derive from our ignorance about particular social phenomena. Third, uncertainty may be an inherent part of all social (and physical) phenomena. Each of these perspectives on the role of chance will be considered below.

Regardless of which of the three perspectives one favors, it is always important that the role of chance be properly taken into account. When formal, quantitative findings are considered, this is sometimes addressed under the heading of *statistical conclusion validity* (Cook and Campbell 1979), and the problem is whether "statistical inference" has been undertaken properly. Thus, just as flipping four heads in a row does not necessarily mean that a coin is biased (because a fair coin will produce four heads in a row once in a while), finding that students exposed to a driver's education course have fewer accidents than those who were not does not necessarily mean that the program was a success. The difference in the number of accidents between students who took a driver's education class and students who did not may have been produced by a chance mechanism analogous to flipping a coin. Unless the role of such chance factors is assessed formally, it is impossible to determine if the program effects are real or illusory.

Similar issues concerning the operation of chance appear in

nonquantitative work as well, although formal assessments of the role of chance are difficult to undertake in such studies. Nevertheless, it is important to ask whether the reported findings rest on observed behavioral patterns that occurred with sufficient frequency and stability to warrant the conclusions that they are not "simply" the result of chance. Good ethnographers often address the role of chance by collecting lots of data, which allows an assessment of whether certain observed phenomena occur so often in particular ways that "the luck of the draw" can implicitly be ruled out.

(1) Having provided a brief taste of the issues, we can return to the three perspectives on chance. Consider first how evaluation data may be collected. *Sampling error* occurs whenever one is trying
(2) to make statements about some population of interest from observations gathered on a subset of that population. For example, one might be studying a sample of students from among those attending a particular school, a sample of teachers from the population of teachers in a particular school system, or even a sample of schools from a population of schools within a city, county, or state. Yet, although it is typically more economical to work with samples, the process of sampling necessarily introduces the prospect that any conclusions based on the sample may differ from conclusions that might have been reached had the full population been studied instead. Indeed, one can well imagine obtaining different results from different subsets of the population.

Although any subset that is selected from a larger population for study purposes may be called a "sample," some subsets may be worse than having no observations at all. The act of sampling must be accomplished according to rational selection procedures that guard against the introduction of selection bias. A biased sample is one in which the statistics calculated will on the average (over many samples) underestimate or overestimate the properties of the population in question (e.g., mean household income in the United States). An unbiased sample is one which the statistics calculated will on the average *not* underestimate or overestimate the properties of the population in question.

A class of such sampling procedures that yield unbiased samples are called *probability samples* in which every element in a population has a known nonzero chance of being selected (Sudman 1976; Kish 1965). Probability samples are difficult to execute and are often quite expensive, especially when dealing with populations that are difficult to locate. Yet there are such clear advantages to such samples, as opposed to haphazard and potentially biased methods of selecting subjects, that probability samples are almost always to be preferred over less rational methods. (See Sudman 1976 for examples of relatively simple and inexpensive probability sampling designs.)

Fortunately, when samples are drawn with probability procedures, disparities between statistics calculated from a sample and the respective population values can only result from the "luck of the draw," and with the proper use of statistical inference, one can place "confidence intervals" around estimates from probability samples, or ask whether a sample estimate differs in a "statistically significant" manner from an assumed population value. In the case of confidence intervals, one can obtain an assessment of how much "wiggle" there is likely to be in one's sample estimates. In the case of significance tests, one can reach a decision about whether a sample statistic (e.g., a mean SAT score) differs from some assumed value in the population (e.g., 600). For example, if the mean SAT score from a random sample of students differs from some national norm, one can determine if the disparities represent statistically significant differences, that is, differences large enough that they could not have occurred easily by chance alone.

A second kind of chance factor associated with data collection stems from the process by which experimental subjects may be *(b)* *assigned* to experimental and control groups. For example, it may turn out that the assignment process yields an experimental group that, on the average, contains brighter students than the control group. This may confound any genuine treatment effects with a priori differences between experimentals and controls; here the impact of some positive treatment such as self-paced instruction will be artificially enhanced because the experimentals were already performing better than the controls.

Much as in the case of random sampling, for experiments in which the assignment to treatment group or control group is undertaken with probability procedures, the role of chance can be taken into account. In particular, it is possible to determine the likelihood that outcome differences between experimentals and controls are statistically significant. If the disparities are statistically significant, chance (through the assignment process) is eliminated as an explanation, and the evaluator can then begin making substantive sense of the results. It is also possible to place confidence intervals around estimates of the treatment effect(s) indicating roughly the likely range of the effects, given that any estimate is subject to random variation.

Chance may enter one's data independent of how the data were collected. Rather, it surfaces even if the total population of interest is studied and no assignment process or sampling procedure is undertaken. Under one conception, chance variation results from the impact of a large number of known unmeasured forces, sometimes called *"perturbations"* or *"errors."* For example, a student's performance on a standardized test may be explained in part by his or her cognitive abilities. In addition, the performance may be affected by how much sleep he or she had the night before, anxiety levels, distractions during the test, whether he or she ate a proper breakfast, a recent quarrel with a sibling, and a host of other factors. Only the first may be understood and measured. The aggregate effect of the rest is the impact of chance. In principle, therefore, the world is deterministic; chance is an artifact of our ignorance. In practice, however, given that at least partial ignorance is a fact of life, the social phenomena are treated as if they contain a significant chance component.

Under a second conception, chance may be an *inherent* property of social life (and the physical world more generally). The mechanisms involved are well beyond the scope of this text (see Berk 1988 for an introduction), but the basic idea is that social life may be in part like the break in a game of eight ball. The curvature of the balls means that very small and seemingly insignificant displacements in where two balls make contact lead to large differences in the angles at which the balls separate.

That is, very small initial differences produce very large consequences. And just as where the balls will stop after the break has a very large element of uncertainty, so does social life. Note that random measurement error may be conceptualized in this fashion because measuring is itself a social process.

Whichever conception one favors, one proceeds in practice with the assumption that, whatever the program processes at work, also at work will be forces that have some impact on outcomes of interest. Typically, these are viewed as a large number of small, random perturbations that on the average cancel one another. Thinking back to the test-taking example above, each neglected factor (e.g., amount of sleep the night before) introduces small amounts of variation in a child's performance, but the aggregate impact is taken to be zero on the average (i.e., their expected value is zero). Yet, because the aggregate impact is only zero on the average, the performance of particular students on particular days will be altered. Thus there will be chance variation in performance that needs to be taken into account. As before, one can apply tests for statistical significance or confidence intervals. One can still ask, for example, if some observed difference between experimentals and controls is larger than might be expected from these chance factors and/or estimate the "wiggle" in experimental-control disparities.

In case it is not clear, statistical conclusion validity speaks to the quality of inferential methods applied and not to whether some result is statistically significant. Statistical conclusion validity may be high or low independent of judgments about statistical significance. (For a more thorough discussion of these and other issues of statistical inference in evaluation research, and statistical inference more generally, see Berk and Brewer 1978; Barnett 1982; Pollard 1986.[4])

Putting It All Together in a Research Design

To briefly summarize our discussion so far, planning an evaluation requires a number of decisions that will affect the validity of the research. First, choices have to be made about how the observed *units* (e.g., people, neighborhoods, schools) will be selected. Probability sampling is one example. Second, decisions have to be made about how *measurement* will be undertaken. For example, an arrest might be measured by an arrest report filed by a police officer. Third, it is also essential to consider how the treatment may be *delivered*. Random assignment is one instance.[5] Plans for undertaking these three activities — selecting the units, measurement, and delivering the intervention — constitute the *research design* of an evaluation.

While the research design speaks to the validity of the study, there are other planning decisions that affect the *relevance* of the evaluation and whether the research design can be effectively *implemented*. In the case of relevance, the intervention must approximate as closely as possible the options in the policy space. In addition, the outcome measures must reflect an outcome that policymakers care about. If the goal of a program is to reduce crime, for example, reducing arrests may or may not be a reasonable proxy (given that many crimes are not reported and that arrests are made for only a fraction of reported crimes). In the worst of all possible worlds, a demonstrable program effect is dismissed because it is the wrong program and the wrong outcome.

In the case of implementation, the research design must be translated into a set of concrete activities that may be undertaken with the resources, personnel, and time available. This is often difficult. For example, it may be impossible to obtain access to police arrest reports needed to measure criminal activity. Or parents may prohibit their children from participating in an experimental sex education class at school. Or overweight individuals may not adhere to the low-calorie diet that was part of the health experiment for which they initially volunteered. We will have more to say about such practical issues later.

The Best Possible Strategy

In the next chapters, the general issues just raised will be addressed in more depth. Before proceeding, however, it is important to stress that practical constraints may intervene in the "real world" of evaluation research, even when an ideal marriage is made between the evaluation questions posed and the empirical techniques employed. Problems of cost, timeliness, political feasibility, and other difficulties may prevent the ideal from being realized. This in turn will require the development of a "second best" evaluation package (or even third best), more attuned to what is possible in practice. Yet, practical constraints do not *in any way* justify a dismissal of technical concerns; if anything, technical concerns become even more salient when less desirable evaluation procedures are employed.

Notes

1. Evaluations are also vulnerable because they rarely have the advantage of a thorough review by social scientists who were not connected to the project. Some argue that, in academic work, research results are typically scrutinized by "peer review" before publication. Important problems are often detected, therefore, before the research is made public. Whether this is true, however, is open to dispute. In any case, in part because of time constraints, evaluations are usually made public without the equivalent of a peer review.

2. Another strategic advantage of attacking a study's methods is that one can capitalize on popular but naive notions of science. It is common for science to be viewed as a fully objective activity that proceeds by certain hard-and-fast rules. If the rules are not followed, the activity is not science. In fact, scientific activities are some complex combination of rules, guidelines, intuition, habit, and social pressure. However, if it can be shown that an evaluation failed to follow some rule (e.g., the subjects were not a representative sample from some designated population), its credibility among many policymakers can be seriously jeopardized.

3. While "nothing" may be one of the options (serving as a comparison group), it cannot be overemphasized that nothing is not nothing (pardon our Zen). At the very least, "nothing" is likely to be the status quo. Moreover, subjects exposed to the status quo may react in a variety of ways (e.g., resentment, depression) if they know that others have been exposed to some innovative intervention. In this instance, the status quo becomes a treatment in the conventional sense; it does something new to subjects.

4. It is important to understand that the issues outlined under "chance" apply to all varieties of evaluation research, whether quantitative in approach or qualitative. However, the methods for dealing with the role of chance are more thoroughly and explicitly developed for quantitative methods.

5. We will have a lot more to say about random assignment later. However, the basic idea is that, if subjects are assigned to experimental and control condi-

tions by the equivalent of a flip of a coin, the experimental and control groups will be, on the average, comparable before the treatment is introduced. This allows for a fair (unbiased) test of the intervention's impact unconfounded with *preexisting* differences between the experimental and control groups.

3

Designing New Programs:
A Chronological Perspective

The Basic Questions

Virtually all evaluation research begins with one or more policy questions in search of answers. Such questions may include how widespread a social problem is, whether any program can be enacted that will ameliorate a problem, whether an existing program is effective, whether an existing program is producing enough benefits to justify its cost, and so on. The following chronological sequence is implied:

1. identification of policy issues;
2. formulation of policy responses;
3. design of programs;
4. improvement of programs;
5. assessment of program impact; and
6. determination of cost-effectiveness.

In practice, sometimes not all six activities are addressed, often with good reason. For example, an evaluation of an ongoing social program such as Social Security might properly begin with the fourth question: "improvement of programs." Less frequently, the questions are addressed in another chronological order. For example, a decision might be made on political grounds to change the Social Security system. Then, the precise nature of those changes would have to be delineated after an empirical analysis of whose needs are not being properly met. However, the six activities provide an initial conceptual framework for what lies ahead.

Fitting the Evaluation Strategy to the Problem

Each of the questions raised by a particular evaluation may be tackled at levels varying in intensity and thoroughness. When great precision is needed and ample resources are available, the most powerful evaluation procedures may be employed. When the occasion demands approximate answers or when resources are in short supply, "rough-and-ready" (and, usually, speedier) procedures can be used. Correspondingly, the answers supplied vary in quality: The findings of some evaluations are more credible than others, but all genuine evaluations produce findings that are better than speculation. They are also likely to produce better findings than conventional wisdom, especially if the wisdom is ideologically congenial. For example, it is commonly believed that the death penalty deters would-be murderers despite study after study failing to find any deterrent effects.[1]

This does not mean that evaluators can use any means available. Rather, they should use the best possible procedures, given available resources and constraints. And this means more than lip service. It is all too common to hear in response to criticism of a slipshod evaluation the very lame excuse that "it was the best we could do under the circumstances," when, in fact, technically superior (and often less wasteful) procedures easily could have been applied.

Given the diversity of policy questions to be answered and enormous variations in available resources, it should not be surprising that there is no single "best way" to proceed. Evaluation research must draw on a variety of perspectives and on a pool of heterogeneous procedures. Thus approaches that might be useful for determining what activities were actually undertaken under some educational program, for instance, might not be appropriate when the time comes to determine whether the program was worth the money spent. Similarly, techniques that may be effective in documenting how a program is functioning on a day-to-day basis may prove inadequate for the task of assessing the program's ultimate impact.

The choice among evaluation methods depends in the first place on the particular question posed; appropriate evaluation techniques must be explicitly linked to each distinct policy question. While this point may seem simple enough, it has been overlooked far too often, resulting in a forced fit between an evaluator's preferred method and particular questions at hand. Another result is an evaluation research literature padded with empty, sectarian debates between warring camps of "true believers." For example, there has been a long and somewhat tedious controversy about whether assessments of the impact of social programs are best undertaken with research designs in which subjects are randomly assigned to experimental and control groups or through theoretically derived causal models of how the program works. In fact, the two approaches are complementary and can be effectively wedded (e.g., Rossi, Berk, and Lenihan 1980; Heckman and Robb 1985).

In the second place, the choice among evaluation methods is conditioned by the resources available and by the amount of precision needed. For example, independent of available resources, a sample of elderly individuals as small as 300 may be sufficient to establish that a significant number of senior citizens have incomes below the poverty line. That is, the sample is large enough to document the existence of a social problem. However, if the program design requires a precise estimate of how many such individuals there are, a sample of several thousand may be needed. Likewise, it is important to consider the ratio of program costs to evaluation costs. Devoting more resources to an evaluation than to the program being evaluated is often overkill and/or political suicide.[2] Nor does it make sense to plan an evaluation that will take several years to complete when the answers it will supply are needed within a few weeks.

Finally, evaluations need to be tailored to the degree of importance of the issue under scrutiny. At one extreme, routine issues for potentially low-impact programs probably do not deserve to be evaluated with any degree of care. For example, it may make very little substantive difference whether soft steel paper clips are superior (or inferior) to plastic paper clips: Hence, it is not worthwhile investing many (if any) resources in evaluating their comparative merits. Yet, such judgments often are not straightforward. While the two kinds of paper clips, for example, may perform similarly, they may have very different environmental consequences. A lot would depend upon the ways in which the two kinds of clips are manufactured and on what happens to them when they are discarded. And, of course, the issue might be extremely salient to paper clip manufacturers.

In contrast, policies dealing with central issues and programs that are very expensive usually deserve the most careful evaluation possible. Thus effort to restrict the use of chloroflourocarbons (CFCs) as propellants in aerosol cans, and in the manufacture of plastic foam cups and refrigerators, should elicit the very best evaluations possible. The switch to other compounds is expensive in developmental costs alone and the political efforts to achieve worldwide cooperation monumental. Moreover, the environmental consequences may border on the incalculable, because the depletion of stratospheric ozone may lead to enormous crop damage. In short, it would be foolish to settle for anything less than the very best.

The Policy Contexts of Evaluation

The six chronological activities listed above can be placed in a richer and broader framework of two *evaluation contexts. Policy and program formulation* is the first, in which questions are raised about the nature and amount of some identified problem, whether appropriate policy actions can be taken, and whether programs that may be proposed are appropriate and effective. In other words, the first context looks to the *future* and what *might* be done. *Examinations of existing policies and programs* is the second, in which attention is directed toward whether extant policies are appropriate and whether current programs have had their intended effects. Thus the second context reviews the *past* to *inform the future.*

Although these two broad contexts, like the earlier six activities, may be regarded as sequential, it often happens that the unfolding policy process may bypass earlier steps. Many major programs have truncated policy formation stages, going straight from the drawing boards of executive agencies or legislatures to full-scale operation. For example, the Head Start and school lunch programs were launched with little program testing beforehand. The issue of whether Head Start was truly effective did not surface until some years after the program had been in place. Similarly, many programs never get beyond the testing stage, because of demonstrated ineffectiveness, political opposition (e.g., contract learning: Gramlich and Koshel 1975), or changes in the policy space (e.g., the negative income tax proposals: Rossi and Lyall 1974).

Looking to the Future: Some Steps in Policy and Program Formulation

Some Background

Proposals for policy changes and new programs presumably arise out of dissatisfaction with the status quo. Sometimes, existing policies and/or programs are not performing as hoped or the problem they were designed to address has changed (or was misread). For example, hardly a week goes by without visible dissatisfaction being expressed about the ways public policy and programs are responding to the "drug problem." Sometimes, new problems arise that were previously unaddressed. Thus current congressional concern about the "greenhouse effect" effectively is new, although scientists have been studying the problem for decades. Ideally, scientific information may be brought to bear on both the nature of the social problem and the potential programmatic responses.

It is important that the previous paragraph not be misunderstood. In particular, we are not implying that the solutions offered by policymakers will necessarily confront the "real" problem in some objective sense. The "real" problem may be far from obvious and certain responses may be immediately seen as impractical or politically unpalatable. For example, is the "real" problem with narcotics the large number of people who are addicted or the current policy that criminalizes the use of narcotics? Some argue that criminalization leads to a variety of problems such as crimes committed to support the purchase of drugs and homicides caused by inner-city gangs fighting to control the drug trade in their neighborhoods. Yet, even if the second definition is preferred, backing decriminalization is at this time political suicide.

Put another way, defining a "social problem" is ultimately a political process whose outcomes do not simply flow from an assessment of available information. Thus, while it would be hard to argue against providing the best possible data on potential areas of need, there is no necessary correspondence between patterns in those data and what eventually surfaces as a subject of concern. For example, in an analysis of pending legislation designed to reduce adolescent pregnancy, the General Accounting Office (GAO 1986) found that none of the legislation addressed teenage fathers. Every proposal treated adolescent pregnancy as if teenage girls could conceive alone. Likewise, recent concerns about water shortages following the dry summer of 1988 typically fail to address the real possibility that water has been priced far too cheaply. The problem, it seems, was not that too much water was used inefficiently, but that the supply of water was inadequate. (See also, Berk and Rossi 1976 for a more thorough discussion of problem definition issues.)

Some final qualifications: In principle and in practice, there is no useful distinction between the formation of new policies and programs and the improvement of existing policies and programs. A proposed improvement is nothing but a proposed change. Correspondingly, evaluation procedures applicable to entirely new policies and programs are suitable for proposed changes in existing policies and programs. Therefore, the discussion that follows does not distinguish between them.

Stage 1:
Defining the Problem

A social problem is a social construction. That is, a condition defined as problematic becomes a problem. Moreover, the particular manner in which the social problems are articulated may have dramatic effects on the kinds of remedies that are suggested. For example, two contending legislative proposals may each address the needs of homeless persons, one identifying the homeless as low-income individuals who have no kin upon whom to be dependent, and the other defining homelessness as the lack of access to conventional shelter. The first definition centers attention on social isolation, while the second concentrates on the availability of affordable housing. It is likely that the ameliorative actions that follow will be different as well. The first might emphasize a program to reconcile estranged individuals with their relatives, while the second might imply a subsidized housing program.

To pursue another example, the presence of hazardous substances in water supplies may be defined either as a use problem or as a production problem. In the first instance, appropriate programs might emphasize how best to educate users about avoiding contaminated water or about purifying water before consumption. The second definition might lead to surveillance of potential polluters and sanctions for violating local pollution ordinances. Note that these two definitions are not contradictory; rather, each highlights an aspect of the problem.

The construction of social problem definitions is, of course, not a task for which evaluators are uniquely trained. Lawyers, judges, staff in administrative agencies, and substantive specialists of various kinds (e.g., hydrologists in the case of water supply) are also trained in how to think about social problems. In addition, there is often a large number of "lay" experts, who are sometimes more sophisticated than the credentialed experts. Yet, there is a special role that evaluators can play in this portion of the evaluation process; they can help all parties think through the substantive and methodological implications of alternative social problem definitions. For example, it is clear that the two definitions of water pollution given above focus on slightly different (albeit overlapping) phenomena, but they also contain clues about the underlying causal factors. Moreover, while the first definition leads to a widespread educational effort for the population at large, the second suggests narrowly focused oversight efforts directed at business firms and municipalities. The former may be more expensive, but also more palatable politically. Yet, it might be easier to monitor the more focused intervention and estimate program impact, perhaps because data are already routinely collected on discharges into local rivers and lakes. In short, judgments about definitional issues often require substantive and methodological knowledge that evaluators often have (or can easily get).

The evaluator can also play an important role by raising for discussion the fit between popular conceptions of the problem and the implicit or explicit definitions included in the legislative or administrative remedies. In this connection, the evaluator would ordinarily refer to legislative proceedings, including committee hearings and floor debates, opinion journals, newspaper and magazine editorials, and other sources in which discussions of the problem may appear. This "homework" can be used to provide policymakers with a wide range of social problem formulations before a final conception is accepted. Otherwise, one risks an irrelevant evaluation.[3]

Evaluators can also be useful in working backward with policymakers from the proposed policies and program to the implied problem definitions. For example, a birth control education program for unwed teenagers may be implicitly defining the problem of teenage pregnancies in terms of illegitimate births. However, this ignores the large number of births experienced by married teenagers. Likewise, an affirmative action program for graduate training in the natural sciences may incorrectly assume that the pool of minority undergraduates properly prepared for graduate work in the natural sciences is as large as the comparable pool of White undergraduates.

Stage 2:
Where Is the Problem and
How Big Is It?

Needs Assessments

Proper design of a public program and projection of its costs require good information on the density, distribution, and overall size of the problem in question. For example, in providing financial support for emergency shelters for homeless persons, it would make a very significant difference if the total homeless population is approximately 3.5 million or approximately 350,000 (both estimates have been advanced). It would also make a big difference whether the problem was located primarily in central cities or whether it can be found in equal densities in small and large places.

An identified problem often is a complex mix of related conditions; planning requires information on that complexity. Retaining the example of homelessness, the proportions of the homeless suffering from chronic mental illness, chronic alcoholism, or physical disabilities need to be known in order to design an appropriate mix of interventions.

It is much easier to identify and define a problem than to develop valid estimates of its density and distribution. For example, a handful of battered children may be enough to establish that a problem of child abuse exists. However, to know how much of a problem exists and where it is located geographically and socially involves detailed knowledge about the population of abused children and their distribution throughout the political jurisdiction in question. Such exact knowledge is ordinarily much more difficult to obtain.

Through their knowledge of the existing literature (consisting of government reports, published and unpublished studies, and limited-distribution reports), and their understanding of which designs and methods lead to credible results, evaluation researchers are in a good position to collate and assess whatever information exists on the issues in question. Equal emphasis is given in the last sentence to both "collate" and "assess": Unevaluated information can often be as bad as no information at all.

For some issues, existing data sources may be of sufficient quality to be used with confidence. For example, information that is routinely collected either by the Current Population Survey or the decennial census is likely to be of adequate quality. Likewise, data available in many of the statistical series routinely collected by federal agencies are often trust-worthy.[4] But when data from other sources are used, it is always necessary to carefully examine how the data were collected. The assessment of data quality is again a task for which evaluators are eminently qualified.

A good rule of thumb is that existing data sources will provide contradictory estimates on any issue. But even chaos can sometimes be reduced to some order. Seemingly contradictory data on the same topic collected by opposing stakeholders can be especially useful for needs assessment purposes. For example, both the Coalition Against Handguns and the National Rifle Association have sponsored sample surveys of the American population concerning their approval or disapproval of gun control legislation. Although the reports issued by the Coalition and the NRA differed widely in their conclusions—with one finding much popular support for more stringent gun control measures and the other the opposite—a close inspection of the data showed that many of the specific findings were nearly identical in the two surveys (Wright et al. 1983). Those findings upon which both surveys agreed substantially could be taken with greater credibility.

In many instances, there may be no existing information that can be used to provide estimates of the extent and distribution of a problem. For example, it is likely that there are no sources of information about how households use pesticides or about the level of popular knowledge concerning how such substances can be safely deployed. Any instance of household pesticide misuse constitutes a problem, but how serious the problem is for, say, households with children present, may be unclear. Moreover, the precise content of the problem may be obscure. Perhaps households lack knowledge about the toxic properties of certain pesticides or, alternatively, they lack knowledge about other ways to control household or garden pests. Ordinarily there are no data sources from which information on such issues can be obtained. Under these circumstances, an evaluator may wish to undertake a preliminary study to estimate the amount and distribution of household pesticide use and knowledge about pesticides' toxic properties.

There are several ways of making such estimates of "need." Perhaps the easiest to undertake, but also the least reliable, is to collect "expert" testimony. Most of the larger estimates of the size of the homeless population are essentially compilations of local "experts'" guesses of the numbers of homeless in their localities. (See U.S. Conference of Mayors 1987.) Another information source that can be reliable, but is often unavailable, is records from organizations that provide services to the population in question. For example, the extent of drug abuse may be extrapolated from the records of persons treated in drug-abuse clinics. Insofar as that the drug-using community is fully covered by existing clinics, such data may be quite accurate.[5]

In many cases, it may be necessary to undertake quite elaborate research in order to assess the extent and amount of some problem. To illustrate, the Robert Wood Johnson Foundation and the Pew Memorial Trust were trying to plan a program for increasing the access of homeless persons to medical care. Although there was ample evidence that serious medical conditions existed among the homeless populations in urban centers, there was virtually no precise information on either the size of the homeless population or the extent of the medical problems in that population.

Hence, the foundations funded a research project to devise technical advances needed in sample survey methods to collect the missing information. The result was a study that influenced most of the subsequent research on homelessness and has led to changes in plans for the 1990 Census, making it possible to arrive at reasonable estimates of the homeless population on a national basis (Rossi, Fisher, and Willis 1986).

Needs assessment research is usually not as elaborate as the pilot research described above. In many cases, straightforward sample surveys can provide most of the information necessary. For example, in planning for educational campaigns to increase public understanding of the risks associated with hazardous substances, it would be necessary to have a good understanding of what the current level of public knowledge is and which population subgroups pose special problems. A national sample survey would provide the necessary information.[6]

The number of local needs assessments covering single municipalities, towns, or counties done every year must now be in the thousands. For example, the 1974 Community Mental Health legislation called for community mental health needs assessments to be undertaken periodically. The 1987 McKinney Act, mandating aid to the homeless, called for states and local communities to undertake needs assessments as the basis for planning programs for the homeless. And social impact statements to be prepared in advance of large-scale alterations in the environment often call for estimates of the numbers of persons or households to be affected or to be served.

The quality of such local needs assessments varies widely but is most likely quite poor on the average. Especially difficult obstacles lie in the requirement to devise valid measurements of relatively subtle social problems (e.g., distrust of food additives, or mental health). For such problems, unusually high-quality surveying methods are essential. Unfortunately, the necessary time, talent, and resources are rarely available at the local level.

Despite our emphasis on things one can count, needs assessments do not have to be undertaken solely with quantitative techniques. *Qualitative* research ranging in complexity from interviewing a few persons through group discussion sessions (as in focus groups) or more elaborate ethnographic fieldwork may also be instructive, especially in getting detailed knowledge of the specific nature of the needs in question. For example, the development of educational campaigns may be considerably aided by qualitative data on the structure of popular beliefs. What, for instance, are the trade-offs people believe exist between the pleasures of cigarette smoking and the resulting health risks?[7]

An especially attractive feature of qualitative approaches is that they are sometimes inexpensive. Certainly, conducting three or four focus group sessions is cheaper than conducting the usual sample survey. Such groups may be especially instructive if groups members are unusually knowledgeable "informants" who have access to information that ordinary citizens would not. For example, problems that an emergency room might be having serving large numbers of low-income patients might be best articulated by emergency room doctors and nurses and by key administrators in that hospital. A haphazard cross-section of citizens would have little concrete information to offer.

However, qualitative approaches can be very expensive if they mean placing several researchers in the field for a number of months. For example, a study of the job training needs of low-income, single parents (primarily women) might require two ethnographers and six months of fieldwork. The cost of the project would then be one person-year of effort from two highly trained anthropologists plus their research expenses (including travel, food, and lodging). The total bill could easily top $100,000.

Although needs assessment research is ordinarily undertaken for the descriptive purpose of developing accurate estimates of the amounts and distribution of a given problem, needs assessments can also yield some understanding of the underlying mechanisms. For example, a search for information on how many high school students study a non-English language may reveal that many schools do not offer such courses; part of the problem is that opportunities to learn foreign languages are insufficient. Or the fact that many primary school children of low socioeconomic backgrounds appear to be tired and list-less in class may be explained by a finding that many ate no breakfast.

Carefully and sensitively conducted qualitative studies are particularly important for uncovering process information of this sort. Thus ethnographic studies of disciplinary problems within high schools may suggest why some schools have fewer disciplinary problems than others, in addition to providing some indication of how widespread disciplinary problems are. The findings on why schools differ might suggest useful ways in which new programs could be designed. Or qualitative research on household energy consumption may reveal that few residents had any information on the energy-consumption characteristics of their appliances. Not knowing how they consume energy, household members can not develop efficient strategies for reducing consumption.

Indeed, the history of ups and downs of public concern for social problems provides many examples of how qualitative studies (e.g., Lewis 1965; Liebow 1967; Riis 1890; Carson 1955), and sometimes novels (e.g., Sinclair 1906; Steinbeck 1939), have raised public consciousness about particular social problems. Sometimes the works in question are skillful combinations of qualitative and quantitative information, as in the case of Harrington (1962), whose *The Other America* contained much publicly available data interlaced with graphic descriptions of the living conditions endured by the poor.

Finally, for program planning purposes, it is often important to be able to project current circumstances into the *future*. A problem that is serious at present, for instance, may be more or less serious years later. Yet, forecasting future trends can be quite risky, especially as the time horizon lengthens. There are a number of technical and practical difficulties, which derive in part from the necessary assumption that the future will be much like the past. For example, a projection of the number of persons aged 18 to 30 a decade later at first blush seems easy to construct; the number of persons of that age 10 years hence is almost completely determined by the current age structure of the population. However, had demographers in central Africa made such a forecast 10 years ago, they would have been substantially off the mark. They would have failed to anticipate the tragic impact of the AIDS epidemic, which is most prevalent among young adults. Projections with longer time horizons would have been even more problematic because trends in fertility as well as mortality would have to have been included.[8]

We are not arguing against forecasting. Rather, we are concerned about uncritical acceptance of forecasts without a thorough examination of how the forecasts were produced. Examining the forecasting assumptions, for example, is a task that can range considerably in complexity. For simple extrapolations of existing trends, the assumptions may be relatively few and easily ascertained. But, even if the assumptions are known, it is often unclear how to determine if the assumptions are reasonably met. For projections developed from multiple-equation computer-based models, examining the assumptions may require the skills of an advanced programmer and the insight of a sophisticated statistician. In any case, all forecasts should be reported as both point and interval estimates. The former is typically a single "best" guess, while the latter is a range of values in which the true (future) value likely lies. Yet, for a large number of forecasting models, it is not apparent how a proper confidence interval may be constructed.

Stage 3:
Can We Do Anything
About the Problems?

Problem-Driven Research

Diagnosis may be the first step on the road to treatment. The second step is understanding enough about the problem and its setting to devise appropriate remedies. That is, knowing a lot about the distribution and extent of a problem does not by itself lead automatically to solutions. In order to design programs, one must call on two sorts of knowledge. First, one needs valid knowledge on the leverage points and interventions useful for changing the distribution and extent of a problem. Second, one needs to know from a variety of sources something about the institutional arrangements that are implicated so that workable policies and programs can be designed.[9]

For example, applied research in microeconomics has shown repeatedly that consumers typically will respond to price. Other things being equal, they will generally buy less of a commodity if its price increases. This lesson can be applied to conservation of all sorts. Yet, it has been virtually impossible in many states to institute marginal cost pricing for water because of political opposition from large agricultural users, who, under existing schemes, are being subsidized by residential and industrial users (Berk et al. 1981).

To take another illustration from water conservation, applied research in social psychology indicates that people who are likely to conserve believe that others drawing on the same resource are conserving as well. Yet, it is unclear how water consumers who believe that other consumers typically are not conserving can be convinced that they are not alone in their support for conservation efforts. The only consumption data they typically see are their own (on their bill). One strategy employed by some water districts in California has been to enclose in each consumer bill a short newsletter reporting aggregate trends in consumption for important segments of the community (Berk et al. 1981).

It cannot be overemphasized that, to construct a program likely to be adopted by an organization, one needs to know how to introduce new procedures that would be undertaken with sufficient effort. Large-scale organizations — schools, factories, social agencies, and the like — are resistant to change, especially when the changes are not reflected in the reward systems. For example, an educational program that is likely to work provides positive incentives for school systems, particular schools and individual teachers. In short, inadequate attention to the organizational contexts of programs is one of the more frequent sources of program implementation failure. Mandating a program for an agency that is insufficiently motivated, poorly prepared, and/or lacking in the necessary skills is a sure recipe for degraded interventions. Indeed, under such circumstances, it is possible that no programs at all will be delivered.

Stage 4:
Developing Promising Ideas into
Promising Programs

Moving from a conception of what may be done to a hypothetical program is the next step, and the act of transforming promising ideas into a set of concrete activities is essentially the practice of art rather than science. Moreover, because the knowledge required is primarily substantive, evaluators have no clear or necessary role. However, evaluators are more likely to make important contributions in the translation of ideas to programs insofar as they have a good understanding of the workings of similarly conceived past programs and of the capabilities of organizations likely to implement the program in question.

As briefly described earlier, for example, during the severe energy crisis of the late 1970s, needs assessments revealed that consumers had little specific knowledge of how their use of electrical appliances affected energy consumption. Of course, nearly every consumer knew that keeping refrigerator doors closed saved electricity and that turning off electrical burners when not being used for cooking would lower electricity consumption. However, few knew that there was wide variation in the energy used by different brands of refrigerators and electrical stoves. Needs assessment research also showed that most consumers were quite concerned about energy costs. In short, there was a reservoir of motivation to adopt energy conservation measures and substantial gaps in popular knowledge about how best to conserve.

Given these circumstances, there were a variety of programs that could have been developed, some resting on pricing changes that would have rewarded consumers for using appliances less during high-demand periods of the day and others based on educational efforts urging consumers to lower their thermostat settings. Furthermore, within each of the these broad categories of programs, there were a variety of specific measures. Pricing schemes, for instance, might be built on the marginal price, the average price, increasing block pricing, and so on. And any pricing scheme based on units of consumption could proceed only if energy consumption could be accurately measured (e.g., by meters). Ideally, the energy consumption for different appliances should be monitored so that, in principle, consumers could determine which appliances were especially inefficient (e.g., toasters) or inappropriately used (e.g., ovens used for heating a room). As a compromise, perhaps energy use could be metered by room. And, finally, means would be necessary to inform consumers about their energy consumption in ways that effectively communicated the consequences of how they used appliances; rapid and accurate feedback would be an essential part of the program. Ideally, appliance-by-appliance breakdowns should be provided.

The point is that programs are a set of *activities* undertaken by individuals and organizations. Specifying these "details" is a very long way from the broad ideas about possible interventions and it requires "nuts-and-bolts" knowledge of past programs and current prospects. In the energy consumption example above, an evaluator would ideally know a lot about a large number of earlier conservation programs and about the day-to-day functioning of the local utility company. Note, however, that such knowledge is primarily substantive and hardly the sole preserve of evaluation researchers.

In contrast, evaluators should feel right at home with *pilot studies*. We know of no clear and compelling definition of a pilot study in a program evaluation context. Perhaps the most useful conception of pilot studies emphasizes the explicitly provisional nature of the intervention being researched. That is, while there is a tentative commitment to a loosely defined program, program developers are consciously agnostic about a host of details on which data may well shed some light. Continuing with the energy conservation example, pilot studies might be undertaken to see how different pricing mechanisms might be instituted and whether there is any evidence that they might work. Thus, if consumers are to pay a higher per-unit price as the amount consumed increases (e.g., under increasing block pricing), there must be some assurance that consumers understand their electric bills and the links between how they use appliances and how much electricity is consumed. These are the kinds of tasks by which evaluators earn their keep.

Likewise, evaluation skills per se are not especially relevant for the translation of broad conceptions of educational television programs into the scripts, lighting, directing, filming, and editing of *Mr. Rogers' Neighborhood*. However, evaluators can play an essential role in the pilot testing (pretesting) of such TV programs. For example, in some circles, educational programs must demonstrate that they can get the attention of their intended audience, be understood by them, and produce a predisposition to act in a desired fashion. Thus pilot versions of new programs are often tested on small audiences whose responses are carefully monitored. Elements of a program that repel audiences, lead to misunderstanding, or lead to undesired behavior can be changed. Then, the program can be finely tuned until pretest audience responses are acceptable.

In practice, useful pilot studies can fall short of full scientific rigor with, for instance, pretest TV audiences that are selected haphazardly. Or pilot studies can involve rigorous research programs that would do a major university proud. Toward the less rigorous side of the continuum, pretesting is routinely undertaken by the Children's Television Workshop, producers of *Sesame Street*. The producers employ volunteer pretest audiences of preschoolers to measure the attention-getting abilities of its TV episodes. The producers watch how closely pretest audiences follow the action of the episode being tested. In addition, the audience is interviewed after each showing to ascertain whether or not the message of the program was understood clearly. Program deficiencies are then rectified, and the process is then repeated until a program acceptable to the producers is finally achieved.

At the other extreme, the Lodge Program developed by Fairweather and his associates employed very rigorous pilot-testing procedures. The goal was to return mental patients to nonin-stitutionalized life in a way that would reduce the chances of being rehospitalized. Drawing upon social science findings about the importance of informal support within small groups, Fairweather and his colleagues took two decades to develop a technique that could be used by most mental hospitals and that was demonstrably effective in lowering the return rates. The development process consisted of a series of randomized field experiments in which version after version of the program was tested until an effective version was achieved.

Thorough pretesting during the development phase can increase the chances that a worthwhile program will emerge. But it is one thing to have a program that works well with test sub-jects and quite another to have a program that will work well with real subjects. For example, a *Sesame Street* episode that does well in a studio atmosphere has none of the competition for attention that exists in an ordinary living room. Indeed, an adult-oriented health information program, *Feeling Good*, that was developed by the Children's Television Workshop did well with pretest audiences but failed to achieve significant audience shares when aired on public TV stations during prime viewing hours. The test audiences in the studios liked the episodes they viewed, but the unconstrained audience preferred programs on other channels that were competing with *Feeling Good*.

Stage 5:
The YOAA Problem

Once a prospective program has been refined through pilot studies, time comes to transport the program to a more realistic operating environment. However, moving from the develop-ment phase to the operational phase usually means transferring responsibility from a research-oriented organization to an oper-ating agency. This leads to the "Can YOAA Do It?" problem: Can "your ordinary American agency" carry out the program with fidelity? Often the YOAA problem has been identified with the character of large-scale bureaucracies, a diagnosis that obscures as much as it illuminates. The issue is whether an operating agency has the appropriately trained personnel, a sufficiently motivating reward system, and the resources to carry out a program at the desired level of fidelity. Asking an already overburdened agency to take on additional work, especially work for which its personnel are not trained, is clearly a recipe for failure. For example, an emergency room program for counseling crime victims, developed in a major Los Angeles hospital, was never implemented because social workers paid by the program were actually used to reduce shortages of social workers in the wards.

In addition, even agencies with the requisite resources and skill may in practice "drop the ball" because of some legitimate confusion, incomplete communication, insufficient follow-through, or a host of effectively unpredictable difficulties. For example, an experimental program in Colorado Springs, Colorado, to test different policing strategies in domestic violence incidents was at first poorly implemented because of a totally unrelated strike threatened by rank and file officers who were seeking bargaining rights for their union. Fortunately, program implementation improved dramatically when the issues underlying the threatened strike were effectively resolved.

Therefore, it is vital to study how programs are *implemented*, and descriptive accounts may be especially valuable. For example, just a few field visits to high schools that were supposed to have in operation a widely publicized program designed to raise the academic motivation levels of poor Black children revealed that the programs existed mainly on paper and in the public relations releases of the main sponsor (Murray 1980). Similarly, careful observations at the sites of the celebrated Cities in Schools Project brought to light that the projects as implemented fell far short of original designs and intentions (Murray 1981).

It is at this point that it may make some sense to initiate *demonstration programs* in which operating agencies attempt to implement the program. Demonstration programs can be viewed as another developmental step when attention is centered on the problems that operating agencies encounter carrying out a program. A prime example is the "administrative experiment" (a misnomer because these demonstrations were not truly experiments) carried out in connection with the proposed housing voucher program. Ten municipalities were selected to work out procedures for administering housing voucher programs in their localities and to carry them out for a period of years. The demonstrations were closely monitored by researchers, who carefully noted all the difficulties each of the ten cities encountered in administering their versions of the housing voucher program (Struyk and Bendick 1981).

Stage 6:
Will a Particular Program Work?

The Effectiveness Issue

After a program has been fine-tuned and its operational kinks ironed out through demonstrations, there still remains the question of effectiveness. To this point, all one has managed to do is document that the program in question can be implemented with sufficient fidelity as a "prototype." It is important to realize that effectiveness goes far beyond implementation and revolves around whether a program produces the changes anticipated. Recall, also, that effectiveness may be relative or marginal, and may take cost into account.

Effectiveness is rarely obvious for at least two reasons. First, it is often difficult to distinguish program effects from other major forces affecting the outcome. We addressed this earlier under internal validity. Second, it is often difficult to distinguish program effects from chance variation, which, as "noise," may mask any program impact. We addressed this earlier in discussing statistical conclusion validity. And both problems are exacerbated by interventions that are typically weak and, for that reason, unlikely to produce strong effects.

Why most interventions are weak raises issues beyond the scope of this book (Rossi 1987). Nevertheless, among the most important explanations is that the social environments in which interventions are likely to be introduced are usually shaped by a large number of forces. Yet the programs introduced rarely address more than one of these. Nutritional behavior, for example, is affected by upbringing, ethnic background, disposable income, local availability of food products, information about nutritional issues, subjective estimates of risks to health and well-being for the nutritional behavior in question, household composition, the nutritional practices of family members and peers, chemical dependencies, and many other influences. Yet programs meant to improve nutrition rarely target more than one of the possible influences. To make matters worse, there appears to be no single developmental stage that, if interrupted, will improve nutritional practices effectively. In short, there are many ways to affect eating habits, but each by itself is a small piece of the picture.

When a promising program has been identified, and a reasonable working version developed, the next step is to see whether the program is effective enough to justify it becoming a routine part of some agency's activities. At this point, we recommend the use of randomized experiments to test the effectiveness of candidate programs. Later, a wider range of design will be discussed when we turn to evaluation of *ongoing* programs. Because the alternatives to random assignment are typically less desirable for causal inference, randomized experiments should be the design of choice when random assignment can be properly implemented. The desirable situation is far more likely to exist when new programs are being developed than when an ongoing program must be assessed, and so we will consider "quasi-experiments" later.

Randomized experiments are desirable (some would say mandatory) because randomly allocating persons (or other units, such as classes) to an experimental group (to which the tested program is administered) or to a control group (from whom the program is withheld) assures that all the factors ordinarily affecting the outcome in question are, on the average, distributed identically across those who receive the program and those who do not.[10]

Therefore, randomization, on the average, prevents the confounding of estimated treatment effects with the impact of other factors that may affect the outcome. As a result, internal validity is enhanced enormously, and the likelihood of reporting spurious causal effects dramatically reduced.

We advocate the use of randomized experiments at this stage in program development because of their scientific merit. (For other assets of randomized experiments, see Berk et al. 1985.) However, this commitment in no way undermines the complementary potential of qualitative approaches such as ethnographic studies, particularly to document why a particular intervention succeeds or fails. For example, in designing educational campaigns based on workshops, qualitative studies can uncover those organizations in which implementation may be most easily achieved. For example, workshops held by employers after 5:00 p.m. may appear to be an efficient strategy except that interviews with employees could reveal that few would remain after hours for any purpose. Indeed, a similar program of proposed workshops to teach better health habits to persons at risk of coronary heart disease failed to attract more than a handful of participants.

Developmental experiments should ordinarily be conducted on a relatively modest scale and are most useful for policy when they test a set of alternative programs that are intended to achieve the *same* effects. For example, it might be useful for an experiment to test several ways of motivating people to have their homes tested for radon because the findings could be used to provide information on the *relative* effectiveness of several attractive (a priori) methods. Likewise, an experiment on a range of policing strategies in domestic violence incidents — arrests, restraining orders, crisis counseling, citations — would be more instructive than an experiment that considers only two alternatives.

There are many good examples of field testing promising programs through randomized experiments. The five income maintenance experiments were devised to test, under varying conditions, the impact of negative income tax plans as substitutes for existing welfare programs (Kershaw and Fair 1976; Rossi and Lyall 1976; Robins 1980; Hausman and Wise 1985). The Department of Labor tested the extension of unemployment benefit coverage to prisoners released from state prisons in a small randomized experiment conducted in Baltimore (Lenihan 1976). Randomized experiments have also been used to test national health insurance plans and direct cash subsidies for housing to poor families.

Perhaps the most extended series of developmental experiments was undertaken by Fairweather and Tornatzky (1977), comprising over two decades of consistent refinement and retesting, and resulting in a replicable, effective treatment that could be implemented under a variety of conditions. In the same spirit, in three cities several extensive tests are currently under way designed to evaluate alternative ways of lowering the incidence of heart disease through improved nutrition. In the environmental area, six alternative approaches to communicating information about radon were tested in New York (Smith et al. 1987). The Minneapolis Spouse Abuse Experiment, which tested three different policing strategies in domestic violence incidents, is being replicated in six new field experiments in six different cities (Berk and Sherman 1988).

Given a program of proven effectiveness, the next question one might reasonably raise is whether the opportunity costs of the program are justified by the gains achieved. Or the same question might be more narrowly raised in a comparative framework: Is Program A more "efficient" than Program B, both otherwise equally acceptable alternate ways of achieving some particular goal?

The main problem is answering such questions centers on establishing a yardstick by which comparisons may be made. For example, would it be more useful to divide the units of achievement gained by dollars, the number of students covered, or the number of classes served by the program? In fact, usually the most convenient way to define efficiency is to calculate cost-effectiveness: the number of dollars spent per unit of output. In the case of *Sesame Street*, for example, two cost-effectiveness measures were computed: (1) dollars spent per child-hour of viewing, a measure of the cost of running the program; and (2) dollars spent per each additional letter of the alphabet learned, a cost-effectiveness measure taking into account increases in learning. Note that the second measure implies knowing the impact of the program, presumably from a formal impact assessment.

The most complicated way of addressing the efficiency question is to conduct a full-fledged benefit-cost analysis in which all of the values of all of the benefits and costs are computed. The ratio of benefits to costs is the benefit-cost ratio of the program. However, relatively few full-fledged benefit-cost analyses have been conducted for social programs because it is difficult to convert all the costs and all the benefits into the same metric. In principle, it is possible to convert into dollars all program costs and benefits. In practice, however, it is rarely possible to do so because of disagreements over the value of various program inputs and outputs. For example, it would be difficult to affix a dollar value to learning an additional letter of the alphabet.

A second problem with full-fledged benefit-cost analyses is that they must consider the long-run consequences of the program in question and the long-run consequences for the next best alternative forgone. This immediately raises the question of how to value, in today's dollars, future returns from some investment. The usual assumption is that current consumption is worth more than future consumption (in part because of delayed gratification), so that a dollar's worth of some commodity today is worth less than a dollar if consumed in the future. This process is called "discounting."

In the context of program evaluation, the future returns (benefits minus costs) of alternative interventions need to be compared *after* discounting. For example, an assessment of a vocational training program in inner-city high schools needs to consider (among many other things) the long-run impact of the program on students' earnings over their lifetimes. At the very least, this means valuing in today's dollars the lifetime earnings of the individuals receiving vocational training and the lifetime earnings of individuals receiving the next best alternative. But, by what fraction should future earnings be discounted? This is always a judgment call about which researchers routinely disagree (Thompson 1980).

In short, complete benefit-cost analyses are typically impractical. However, the attempt itself is often useful because it forces policymakers to confront the painful fact that all social programs have opportunity costs in both the short and the long run. In addition, phrasing program outcomes in cost-effectiveness terms is often a handy method for addressing the trade-offs between alternative programs.

Practical Developmental Evaluation Approaches

If all of the research activities described in the preceding pages were undertaken for each and every proposed program or policy shift, the pace of change in American public programs would be appreciably slowed. Thus, while one must admire the devotion, care, and diligence of Fairweather and his colleagues, when the Lodge approach had finally been perfected, psychopharmacological developments and the community mental health movement had so drastically changed the treatment of mental health patients that the Lodge approach had become largely irrelevant.[11] While Fairweather and his associates labored carefully and at great length to perfect the Lodge approach, the content of policy space had shifted to highlight other concerns about the treatment of the mentally ill.

Clearly, practical approaches to program development have to take into account all the constraints on time and resources that are ordinarily confronted. Decades-long development efforts may be the "right" way, but the practical way must deliver the best possible information in a timely fashion. There are no hard-and-fast guidelines about how best to proceed, although a few broad principles may be stated.

In general, judgments about whether to evaluate a program, and about how thorough that evaluation should be, should rest, at least in principle, on a rough benefit-cost ratio for the proposed *evaluation*. That is, one must place some value on the *information* that could be obtained under different evaluation designs. Other things being equal, the greater the potential impact of the proposed program — whether it succeeds *or* fails — the more carefully it should be evaluated. This means that programs that promise to be costly, that may have adverse and widespread effects, or that deal with the central, gnawing problems of society probably deserve the best possible evaluation. Programs in which the consequences of an ineffective program are slight may typically warrant far less thorough attention. Indeed, there is no doubt that some programs need not be scrutinized at all. However, before proceeding, it is vital to factor in what kinds of evaluations are feasible, how credible their results are likely to be, and what each would cost to undertake. A very important program, such as Social Security, may be prohibitively expensive to evaluate persuasively. Alternatively, an evaluation of a community's efforts to reduce bicycle accidents, by instituting inspections of bicycles ridden to local schools, may produce lots of useful information per dollar of cost.

Finally, the evaluative activities in support of program development have been described above as a set of procedures arrayed over time. We emphasize again that this need not be the case. A set of experiments conducted simultaneously on several alternative programs can reduce the total time needed to arrive at useful conclusions. Demonstrations of programs can be used for fine-tuning purposes. Randomized experiments may be forgone when there are very strong indications of effectiveness from nonexperimental evidence. While there is an expositional logic to the chronology presented and a thoroughness that follows when each stage is executed in the order proposed, we are offering no recipe. Evaluation practitioners in real time and on site will always have to make judgment calls.

Notes

1. In this case the "treatment" is an execution and the "control" is a very long prison term.

2. However, one must carefully judge what is at stake. For example, while the cost of an evaluation may loom large compared to the cost of the particular program under consideration, the evaluation findings may have vital implications for many more programs and for a larger program. In the context of the universe

of programs potentially affected, the evaluation budget may be relatively small.

3. In our experience, as the problem definition is being constructed, it is vital for evaluators to make explicit what is going on: important options are being foreclosed. Policymakers should be constantly reminded that there are opportunity costs to their decisions. Otherwise, one risks having policymakers later dissociate themselves from the evaluation, claiming that they were misled when the evaluation was designed.

4. There are, unfortunately, exceptions. For example, it is widely acknowledged that the U.S. census undercounts the number of Blacks and Hispanics. For the nation as a whole, the undercount is relatively small and for most purposes it can be ignored. However, for some jurisdictions with large populations of Blacks and Hispanics, the undercount translates into substantial losses of federal funds (because many programs are tied to the size of particular populations). This led to a lawsuit by the State of New York in which statistical adjustments for the undercount have been proposed (Ericksen and Kadane 1985). In short, how good the data have to be always depends on how those data will be used.

5. It is also the case that, if drug-abuse clinics did cover all or most of the drug-abusing population, drug-abuse treatment programs might not be an issue. Hence, to the extent that a problem is being adequately addressed by existing programs, data from such programs may be useful, but that is not the typical situation in which data are needed.

6. There are many national survey organizations that have, under contract, the capability to plan, carry out, and analyze such surveys. In addition, it is often possible to add questions to an existing national survey, possibly reducing costs. It should be noted that, for surveys of a given sample size, national surveys are just slightly more expensive than local surveys.

7. On the other hand, when the time comes to assess the extent of the problem, there is usually no substitute for formal quantitative procedures. Stated a bit starkly, qualitative procedures are likely to be especially effective in determining the nature of the need. Quantitative procedures are, however, essential to determine the extent of need.

8. There are a number of other problems forecasters face. For example, suppose that a utility company wanted to forecast the demand for electricity 10 years in the future. Because there is obviously a strong relationship between the number of residential, industrial, and agricultural customers and the demand for electricity, knowing the numbers of each kind of customer will provide a basis for instructive forecasts. However, those numbers would have to be forecasted themselves, because the number of customers affects demand contemporaneously. These and other problems are discussed in a broad social science context by Berk and Cooley (1987).

9. This conception of policy-driven research apparently causes considerable misunderstanding about the relationships between basic and applied social research. Policy-driven research tries to determine how changes in policy can affect the phenomenon in question. In contrast, knowledge about the phenomenon per se (the province of basic disciplinary concerns) may have no ready links to what can be done about it. For example, a study finding convincingly that violent criminals often were abused as children does not by itself lead to rehabilita-

tion programs for violent criminals or to concrete interventions in the homes of abused children. However, such a study might stimulate ideas for the kinds of policy-driven research necessary to develop sensible responses. That is, basic research may provide general clues about where and how to intervene.

10. Randomization also means that the assumptions for routine significance tests are likely to be met.

11. Fairweather's efforts were not totally in vain. The basic understanding gained about what is needed to sustain chronically mentally ill patients outside institutions has made important contributions to the treatment of deinstitutionalized former patients.

4

Examining Ongoing Programs: A Chronological Perspective

Once a program has been enacted and is functioning, one of the main questions is whether the program is functioning properly. Attention is not directed to whether the program is achieving its intended effects but to whether the program is operating day to day as expected. Often explicit is a comparison between the program as designed and the program as it is actually implemented. For example, even well-planned programs often have to be fine-tuned in the first few months of operation. (Indeed, estimates of effectiveness, therefore, should be made only when any necessary "shakedown period" is over.)

Stage 1:
Is the Program Reaching the
Appropriate Beneficiaries?

Achieving appropriate coverage of beneficiaries is often problematic. Sometimes a program is so poorly designed that it simply does not reach significant portions of the total intended beneficiary population. For example, an educational program designed to reach intravenous drug users through community

institutions such as churches and schools may simply miss its
target population, which does not use the community institutions. A program to provide food subsidies to children who
spend their days in child-care facilities may fail to reach a large
proportion of such children if regulations exclude child-care
facilities that are serving fewer than five children. A very large
proportion of children who are cared for during the day outside
their own households are cared for by women who take a few
children into their homes (Abt Associates 1979).

A thorough needs assessment of child-care problems would
have revealed that such a large fraction of child care was furnished
by small-scale vendors and, hence, should have been taken into
account in drawing up administrative regulations. However, the
needs assessment might not have been thorough enough. In addition, patterns of the problem may change over time, sometimes
in response to the existence of a program itself. For example, it
is quite likely that the existence of shelters for battered women
increases the demand for shelters. Among other things, shelters
validate the option of leaving oppressive living arrangements.
Another example concerns the labeling of consumer products.
Labels printed in extremely small type or that use professional
jargon may satisfy agency regulations; they may also be ignored
by most consumers. The labeling program simply does not reach
many of its intended beneficiaries. In short, it is important to
review from time to time how many of the intended beneficiaries
are in fact being covered by a program.

Experience with social programs over the past two decades
has shown that there are few, if any, programs that achieve full
coverage or even near full coverage of intended beneficiaries,
especially where coverage depends on actions that must be
undertaken by prospective beneficiaries. Thus not all persons
who are eligible for Social Security payments actually apply for
them; estimates indicate that up to 15% of all eligible
beneficiaries never apply. AFDC programs only reach about half
of the families who are eligible. Some intended beneficiaries
may not be reached because facilities for delivering the services
are not accessible. A single job training program for all of the

State of Iowa that is located solely in Dubuque effectively does not exist for individuals who live more than 50 miles away. There is also another side to the coverage problem. Programs may extend benefits to persons or organizations that were not intended beneficiaries. Such unwanted coverage may be impossible to avoid because of the ways in which the program is delivered. For example, although *Sesame Street* was designed primarily to reach disadvantaged children, it was attractive to advantaged children and to many adults. There is no way to keep anyone from viewing a television program once broadcast (nor is it entirely desirable to do so in this case), and hence a successful TV program designed to reach some specific group of children may reach many others as well (Cook et al. 1975).

Although the unintended viewers of *Sesame Street* are reached at no additional cost to broadcasters, there are times when "unwanted" coverage may severely drain program resources. For example, while Congress may have wished to provide educational experiences to returning veterans through the GI Bill and its successors, it was not clear whether Congress had in mind the subsidization of the many new proprietary educational enterprises that came into being primarily to supply "vocational" education to eligible veterans. Or, in the case of the bilingual education program, many primarily English-speaking children were found to be program beneficiaries because some school systems discovered that the special bilingual classes were an excellent place to tuck away their trouble-making English-speaking students.

Studies designed to measure coverage are similar in principle to those discussed under needs assessment studies earlier. For example, a utility company might survey its customers to determine who is taking advantage of an advertised rebate for installing better home insulation. Or a telephone company might review its own records to see how many of its customers are taking advantage of "lifeline" rates. Or a university might examine its admissions records to determine if affirmative action programs are being applied inappropriately to non-covered minority groups (e.g., Asian Americans). Perhaps the main difference between coverage studies and needs assessments is that for the former there will more likely be systematic records on which to build. That is, the existence of a functioning program often implies the existence of program records with useful information.

Stage 2:
Is the Program Being
Properly Delivered?

Program Integrity Research

It is far easier to describe a program than deliver it. Especially when program services depend heavily on the ability to recruit and train appropriate personnel, to retrain existing personnel, or to undertake significant changes in standard operating procedures, it is sometimes difficult to implement the intervention as designed. And one cannot always rule out incompetence or outright corruption. But whatever the reason, a program that is not delivered as it was intended subverts the earlier developmental effort and spends money on false pretenses.

Several examples may highlight the importance of program integrity. Although informational pamphlets on proper nutrition can be provided to medical personnel, pharmacies, and hospitals, the distribution of such literature to patients is always problematic. Properly motivating personnel to add the distribution of pamphlets to their existing duties is necessary but difficult to accomplish. And if the pamphlets are not delivered, there is no program. Likewise, when an educational program on birth control requires that special equipment be used, as in the case of the distribution of video- and audiocassettes, delivery of the program can be made problematic. In some instances, for instance, an assumption that schools have the requisite equipment may be false.

In other cases, the anticipated services are delivered, but in diluted form. For example, a supplementary reading instruction program may be designed for an average of two instructional hours per student per week. However, in practice, 30 minutes of the program may be delivered on the average. The 75% reduction may lower reading gains proportionally, in which case the program's impact may be trivial. Or worse, the 75% reduction may drop the program below a threshold at which any gains occur.

Program integrity is often a particular problem in "loosely coupled" organizations in which the lines of authority are unclear or in which the lines of authority mean little in practice. Academic departments in universities are an excellent example. The professional autonomy given to professors and the ideal of academic freedom mean that department chairs often have little control over what is taught in classrooms. Many human service organizations have similar problems: hospitals, police departments, courts, welfare departments, and secondary schools. In all such organizations it is difficult to control what is occurring at the point of service delivery because of the discretion and autonomy given to service workers. To take another example, despite the threat of AIDS and other blood-transmitted diseases, it is often difficult to get emergency room nurses to always use surgical gloves when handling patients.

Evaluation research designed to measure what is being delivered may be simple or complex. Thus it may be very easy to learn from hospitals how many persons are served each week in their various outpatient services, but very difficult to learn precisely what transpires in the interactions between medical personnel and patients. For example, if one is interested in the kinds of information provided by physicians and nurses in outpatient care, one would have to undertake an in-depth observational study that might well be very expensive to implement on a large scale. As another illustration, consider an evaluation of efforts to teach literacy as part of vocational training. One key question might be whether a particular pedagogical approach was being employed as promised. If only about six classes were being studied, two full-time observers would probably be needed to do classroom observation. In addition, there is always the possibility that the presence of observers may alter the behaviors of teachers and students.

One of the best examples of systematic studies in difficult-to-observe situations is Reiss's (1971) study of police-citizen encounters. Research assistants were assigned to ride with police on patrol and to systematically record each encounter between the police and members of the public. Reiss's study provides basic descriptive accounts of how such encounters are generated, how behavior of citizens affected police responses, and so on.

A recent example of an excellent implementation study examines the mental hospitals that serve the Chicago metropolitan area (Lewis et al. 1987). The main problem was to describe how the legislation and rules for involuntary commitment to mental hospitals in place since the 1970s were working out in practice. The researchers discovered that fewer than 1% of the patients admitted over a year's time were involuntarily committed. Observing the court procedures, they found that many persons brought to the attention of the police because of their bizarre or aggressive behavior were offered the choice of voluntary commitment for up to 30 days or being involuntarily committed for 60 days or more. The courts and prosecutors offered these alternatives because involuntary commitment involved lengthy procedures that could appreciably reduce the number of cases the court could process. Given the choice, most persons brought in under complaint choose the more lenient alternative. These practices averted what might potentially have been a very high burden on the courts and prosecutors.

To fine-tune a program, it may not be necessary to collect data on a large scale. It may not matter, for instance, whether a particular implementation problem occurs frequently or infrequently, because it is not desirable for it to occur at all. Thus small-scale, qualitative observational studies may be most fruitful for program fine-tuning. For example, if qualitative interviews with welfare recipients reveal any instances in which husband-wife separations were undertaken solely for the purpose of retaining or increasing benefit eligibility, there might be sufficient evidence for revision of the program eligibility rule.

Programs that depend heavily on particular personnel for delivery and/or that involve complicated activities and/or that call for individualized treatments for beneficiaries are especially good candidates for careful and sensitive fine-tuning research. Such programs imply that the unique characteristics of program personnel coupled with the unique characteristics of beneficiaries effectively determine what is delivered. Because it is impossible to standardize the program, it is difficult to control what is delivered. Thus individualized human services are especially problematic. (See Fairweather and Tornatzky 1977 for an outstanding example.)

Stage 3:
Are the Funds Being
Used Appropriately?

Fiscal Accountability

The accounting profession has been around considerably longer than has program evaluation; procedures for determining whether program funds have been used responsibly and as intended are well established and, hence, are not problematic. However, assessments of fiscal accountability cannot substitute for the studies mentioned above. Proper use of funds does not necessarily imply that program services are being delivered as intended. Conventional accounting categories used in fiscal audits are ordinarily sufficient to detect fraudulent expenditure patterns, but they may be insufficiently sensitive to detect whether services are being delivered to appropriate beneficiaries at the recommended levels. As described earlier, for instance, just because salaries of emergency room social workers were paid as promised did not mean that the social workers were delivering the promised services. Recall that the social workers were commonly used on the wards instead of in the emergency room. In this light, it is instructive that the General Accounting Office has set up a separate section, called the Program Evaluation and Methodology Division, one of whose major roles is to instruct GAO personnel in appropriate evaluation procedures and to undertake evaluations of programs upon the request of Congress.

It is also important to keep in mind that the definition of costs under accounting principles differs from the definition of costs used by economists. For accountants, a cost reflects conventional bookkeeping entries such as out-of-pocket expenses, historical costs (i.e., what the purchase price of some item was), depreciation, and the like. Accountants focus on the value of current stocks of capital goods and inventories of products coupled with "cash flow" concerns. When the question is whether program funds are being appropriately spent, the accountants' definition will suffice.

However, economists stress opportunity costs defined in terms of what is *given up* when resources are allocated to particular purposes. More specifically, opportunity costs reflect the *next best* use to which the resources could be put. For example, the opportunity cost of raising teachers' salaries by 10% may be the necessity of forgoing the purchase of a new set of textbooks. While opportunity costs may not be especially important from a cost-accounting point of view, they become critical when cost-effectiveness or benefit-cost analyses of programs are undertaken. We will have more to say about these issues later.

The three evaluation tasks just discussed are directed mainly to how well a program is functioning. Whether or not a program is effective is a different question, to which answers are not easily provided. Essentially, one must determine whether or not a program is achieving its goals over and above what would be expected if the program did not exist. We turn to that enterprise now.

Many evaluators consider the effectiveness question to be quintessentially evaluation. We suspect that this derives in part from the laboratory roots of many evaluation research techniques. In the laboratory, the treatment and control conditions are usually under the control of the researcher and, as a consequence, are not problematic. The researcher knows what was being delivered to whom. The "real" question, therefore, becomes whether the treatment had any impact. However, social programs are not launched in laboratories, and program content is often the critical issue. Indeed, one could argue that, unless there are ways to determine precisely what was delivered to whom, program impact is irrelevant: What good is an effect without knowing its cause?

Suppose, for example, that one wanted to evaluate efforts to introduce literacy training into vocational training classes. Also suppose that vocational trainees are assigned at random to two classrooms, one of which is to teach the usual vocational content and one of which is to integrate literacy and vocational training. Finally, suppose that, while there are absolutely no data on what went on in the two classrooms (either from observation, accounts from students, accounts from teachers or other sources), later reading scores for the integrated curriculum are far higher than for the vocational curriculum alone. That is, there is convincing evidence of program impact. However, without knowing about treatment content, what could possibly be done with the results? It is impossible, for instance, to use these results to justify routinizing the program, because no one but the students and teachers have any idea what the program is. Routinize what?

This illustration conveys why, in our view, questions about how a program is functioning logically precede questions about program impact. An impact assessment is a waste of time unless the intervention is understood. Thus there is certainly no justification for interpreting every evaluation task in effectiveness terms, as some evaluators have done in the past, spurred by imprecise requests for help from policymakers and administrators.

Once the treatment is well documented, however, the success or failure of that program is quite properly addressed. The proverbial "bottom line" is always whether the program "works." We turn, then, to ways in which program effectiveness may be empirically examined.

Stage 4:
Can Effectiveness Be Estimated?

The Evaluability Question

The effectiveness of a program that has gone through the stages described earlier in this chapter should, in principle, be an answerable empirical question. Put a bit more cautiously, an impact assessment will not be precluded. But there are many human services programs that present problems for effectiveness studies because one or more of the stages described earlier was neglected or handled poorly. Perhaps most important, an impact assessment is impossible without well-formulated program objectives. For example, a program designed to increase learning among certain groups of schoolchildren through the provision of supplemental per capita payments to schools is not evaluable without further specification of goals. "Increase learning" is hardly very specific. One would need to know such things as what sort of "learning" was to be included and what a nontrivial "increase" entailed.

Even biomedical experiments are not immune to vague goals.[1] Freedman and Zeisel (1988) describe testing the claims that a certain chemical is alleged to increase the risk of cancer, assuming that this claim may be evaluated with a randomized experiment using mice as subjects. A perplexing question soon presented itself: How should they define the outcome variables? Carcinogens are often rather specific in their impact; one may be associated with cancer of the liver and another with cancer of the lungs. For an experiment at hand, which cancers should be counted? If, for example, all cancers are counted, an apparent finding of "no effect" may be misleading. Small but important effects for a *particular* kind of cancer may be lost in the "noise" when all tumors are aggregated. In other words, the outcome should have been stated in terms of the particular kinds of cancers anticipated, not cancer in general.

Clarifying goals can often be accomplished by helping program personnel to articulate them. This may mean several hours of conversations over a number of weeks. For example, a Bay Area program of workshops on domestic violence designed for judges had as its initial goal "making judges more sensitive to family violence cases." Did this mean changing sentencing patterns, providing through counselors emotional support for victims, reducing the number of continuances (which are very hard on victims), or what? It took several meetings among the evaluator, agency personnel, and the agency's advisory board before the program's goals were properly clarified. Yet this step was absolutely essential.

A second criterion for evaluability is that program content be well specified. Thus a program "encouraging innovation" to make health education agencies more effective is not amenable to an impact assessment. In addition to vague goals, the means for reaching the goals are unclear. "Innovation" is not a method but a means of proceeding. And because anything new is an innovation, the health education program may encourage the temporary adoption of a wide variety of techniques likely to vary widely from site to site. In short, it must be clear what the intended intervention is.

Third, a program's impact may be estimated only if it is possible to credibly approximate what would have happened to the targeted recipients in the absence of the program. (See our earlier discussion of causality.) For example, randomized experiments are a powerful means to make causal inferences about the impact of social programs, but, more generally, constructing comparison groups of various kinds, whether by random assignment or not, is usually essential. Hence, a program that is universal in its coverage and that has been going on for some period of time is very difficult (perhaps impossible) to evaluate for effectiveness. One cannot evaluate, therefore, the effectiveness of the public school systems in the United States because one cannot find American cities, towns, counties, and states that do not have (or recently have not had) public school systems.

To illustrate further the need for comparisons, a county in Northern California wanted an impact assessment of prosecutorial efforts to increase the likelihood that serious drug offenders would be sanctioned severely and swiftly. One of the evaluation outcomes was citizens' fear of crime; presumably, swift and severe sanctions would bring down the crime rate, at least for drug-related offenses. Unfortunately, the evaluation was requested after the program began, and no pretest of citizen attitudes was possible. Without a pretest, it is simply impossible to tell whether the program possibly made any difference.

Finally, effectiveness evaluations are often the most difficult kinds of evaluations, requiring highly trained personnel and, sometimes, large sums of money. Thus it is silly to plan evaluations of program impact unless there are sufficient resources and unless appropriately trained professionals are available. Unfortunately, legislatures and administrators have often mistakenly required effectiveness evaluations from agencies that are not prepared to undertake them, often assuming as well that the costs would be modest (Raizen and Rossi 1981). For example, recent federal legislation has required the National Institute of Justice to undertake an impact assessment of the large grants awarded to states and counties to "fight drugs." Yet, there was no accompanying appropriation and, at least informally, there were unrealistically high expectations about what could be learned.

There are no hard-and-fast rules about how much an effectiveness evaluation should cost or about how much skill may be needed. However, sometimes a useful *starting point* for discussions of research costs is to ask that the equivalent of at least 1% of the program's operating budget be available for program evaluation. For the requisite research skills, it is always helpful if the individuals who will be doing the evaluation have *successfully* done such research in the (recent) past; a track record is very important, far more important than formal credentials.

Techniques have been developed (Wholey 1977) to determine whether a program is evaluable in the senses discussed above. Decision makers are well advised to commission such studies as a first step rather than to assume that all programs can be evaluated. Evaluability assessments essentially determine whether there are program goals that are sufficiently well articulated, whether the program is sufficiently clear and uniformly delivered, and whether the requisite resources are available.

Finally, it may be worth mentioning that questions of evaluability have in the past been used to justify "goal-free" evaluation methods (e.g., Scriven 1972; Deutscher 1977). The goal-free advocates have contended that, because many of a program's aims evolve over time, the "hypothetico-deductive" approach to impact assessment (Heilman 1980) is at best incomplete and at worst misleading. In our view, impact assessment necessarily requires some set of program goals; and whether they are stated in advance and/or evolve over time does have important implications for one's research procedures (Chen and Rossi 1980). In particular, evolving goals require far more flexible research designs (and researchers). In other words, there cannot be such a thing as a "goal-free" impact assessment. At the same time, we have stressed above that there are other important dimensions to the evaluation enterprise in which goals are far less central. For example, a sensitive monitoring of program activities can proceed productively without any consideration of ultimate goals. Thus goal-free evaluation approaches can be extremely useful as long as the questions they can address are clearly understood.

Stage 5:
Did the Program Work?
The Effectiveness Question

As discussed above, any assessment of whether or not a program "worked" necessarily assumes that it is known what the program was supposed to accomplish. For a variety of reasons, enabling legislation establishing programs often appears to set relatively vague objectives for the program, making it necessary (as discussed above) to develop specific goals during the "design phase." Goals for such general programs may be devised by program administrators through consideration of social science theory, past research, and/or studies of the problem that the program is supposed to ameliorate.

In whatever way goals may be established, the important point is that it is not possible to determine whether a program worked without developing a limited and specific set of criteria for establishing the condition of "having worked." Beyond clear goals, therefore, there needs to be a rather clear concept of "how good is good enough." For example, it would not have been possible to develop an assessment of whether *Sesame Street* "worked" without having decided that its goals were to foster reading and number-handling skills. But, once that was determined, there still remained the vital question of how large a gain in performance was to be called a success. A quarter of a grade level? A half of a grade level? Two grade levels?

In other words, without specificity about the *size* of the program effect required, program evaluators are shooting at a moving target. Without such specificity, there will not be enough information about the effects being sought to properly inform a number of critical design decisions. For example, there will be no way to determine the necessary sample size because the appropriate sample size determination depends in part on the size of the effect one is trying to find; smaller anticipated effects require larger samples. Likewise, it will be very difficult to decide how to measure the outcome variable. Again, the amount of precision depends on the size of the effect being sought. Then, when the time comes for analysis, unnecessary uncertainty is compounded. For example, one may well lose the ability to do significance tests designed maximally to address whether the program worked as hoped (e.g., Goodman and Royall 1988). One could not, for instance, define the null hypothesis in terms of the amount of effectiveness required for the program to be called a success. Finally, the evaluation report will be subject to a large number of ad hoc interpretations because the definition of success will often be person-specific. One person's success may be another person's failure. That is, two individuals examining the same empirical results may legitimately draw contradictory conclusions.[2]

Assuming, however, that "success" is properly defined, one must still respond to the reality that programs never succeed or fail in absolute terms. Success or failure is always relative to some bench mark. Hence an answer to the question: "Did the program work?" requires consideration of the question: "Compared with what?"

The "compared to what?" question is by now an old friend, introduced most thoroughly when we earlier considered impact assessment of new programs. Recall that impact assessments for new programs were generally best undertaken with randomized field experiments. By and large, randomized designs are still the method of choice, although for ongoing social programs, random assignment faces a number of additional practical obstacles. For example, program recipients may feel entitled to a service they have been receiving for some time. Consider, for instance, the availability of unmetered water in a number of rural communities. The switch to metered water would generate a public outcry (and has in some locales), perhaps especially if coupled with random assignment. Access to water from local aquifers, rivers, streams, and lakes is, in many areas, part of the rights that historically have come with ownership of land.

In short, it is time to briefly review alternatives to randomized experiments; we must allow for the possibility that comparisons to the intervention may involve non-randomly constructed groups of various kinds. Note, in addition, that while the alternatives are likely to be especially relevant to impact assessments of ongoing programs, they may also be used (as a second choice) in impact assessments of new programs.

The development of appropriate comparisons can proceed along at least three dimensions: (1) comparisons across different subjects, (2) comparisons across different settings, and (3) comparisons across different times. In the first instance, one might compare different sets of persons, trying to hold constant the setting and when the study is undertaken. In the second instance, one might compare the performance of the same set of persons in different settings—such as at home and at work (necessarily at two different points in time). In the third instance, one might compare the same students in the same setting but at different points in time.

Consider as an example different levels of aggregation involved in school settings (individual students, classes, and schools) and the time structuring of schooling (class periods, terms, and academic years).[3] As Table 4.1 indicates, it is possible to mix these three fundamental dimensions to develop a wide variety of comparison groups. For example, comparison group C_2[4] varies both the subjects and the setting although the time is the same. Or comparison group C_6 varies the subjects, the setting, and the time. However, with each added dimension by which one or more comparison groups differ from the experimental group, the number of threats to the validity of the resulting effectiveness estimates necessarily increases. For example, the use of comparison group C_4 (different setting and different time period) requires that assessment of program impact simultaneously take into account possible confounding factors associated with such things as changes in student background and motivation and such things as the "reactive" potential of different classroom environments.

As an illustration of the difficulties that often follow in the absence of random assignment, consider the evaluation (Robertson 1980) of the effectiveness of high school driver education programs in which the goal was to reduce automobile accidents among 16- to 18-year-olds. Despite sympathy for the programs, the state legislature decided not to provide any funding. In response, some school districts dropped driver education from their high school curriculum and some retained it. Two sets of comparisons were possible: (1) accident rates for persons of the appropriate age range in the districts that dropped the program computed before and after the program was dropped, and (2) accident rates for the same age groups in the districts that retained driver education compared with the accident rates in districts that dropped the driver education program.

It was found that the accident rates were significantly lower in those districts that dropped the program, a finding that might lead one to believe that the program *increased* the risk of accidents, perhaps because young people were enticed to obtain licenses earlier. However, internal validity in this instance depends on considerable knowledge about the process by which some school boards dropped the program. In most cases, school

Table 4.1 A Typology of Comparison Groups

| | Same Subjects | | Different Subjects | |
	Same Setting	Different Setting	Same Setting	Different Setting
Same Time	XX[a]	XX[b]	C_1	C_2
Different Time	C_3	C_4	C_5	C_6

a. No comparision is possible.
b. Although logically possible, it is not sensible for human subjects.

boards apparently dropped the program because of financial considerations. If (and only if) one can accept that local financial concerns were unrelated to the number of automobile accidents in the past, then (the unfortunate) inferences about the impact of the driver education program may be taken seriously.[5]

Of course, randomization will, on the average, eliminate confounding influences in the estimation of impact. On grounds of analytic simplicity alone, it is easy to see, therefore, why so many expositions of impact assessment strongly favor research designs based on random assignment. As noted earlier, however, random assignment is often impractical or even impossible. And even when random assignment is feasible, its advantages rest on randomly assigning a relatively large number of subjects. To randomly assign only two schools to the experimental group and only two schools to the control group, for example, will not allow the average equivalence between experimentals and controls to materialize.[6] Consequently, one is often forced to attempt statistical adjustments for initial differences between experimental and comparison subjects. Whether or not such adjustments succeed is always questionable.

What about using statistical controls? Unfortunately, appropriate statistical adjustments (in the absence of randomization) through multivariate statistical techniques require a number of assumptions that are almost impossible to meet fully in practice. For example, it is essential that measures of all confounding influences be included in a formal model of the program's impact, that their mathematical relationship to the outcome be properly specified (e.g., a linear additive form versus a multiplicative form), and that the confounding influences be measured without error. Should any of these requirements be violated, one risks serious bias in any estimates of program impact.

While we will have a bit more to say about multivariate statistical adjustments later, suffice it to say now that there is a growing consensus among statisticians that social scientists of various stripes have routinely pushed statistical procedures well beyond where they are designed to go. (See, for example, the Summer 1987 issue of *The Journal of Educational Statistics*.)

Statistical procedures have far too often been applied to data that are not even remotely appropriate, relying on assumptions that have virtually no justification. Coming under particular criticism is the use of "structural equation models" (especially with "latent" variables),[7] which regularly outstrip social science data and theory. At this juncture, perhaps the best advice is that fancy statistics is no substitute for random assignment, and statistical analyses should be simple and as close to the data as possible. For example, multivariate matching, when feasible, may be superior to statistical adjustments (often based on techniques such as multiple regression) because matching assumes no functional form between the explanatory/control variables and the outcome (Rosenbaum and Rubin 1985).[8]

It is sometimes possible either to solve or to partially bypass comparison group problems by resorting to some set of external criteria as a baseline. For example, it is common in studies of desegregation or affirmative action programs to apply various measures of equity as a "comparison group" (Baldus and Cole 1977). Thus an assessment of whether schools in Black neighborhoods are being funded at comparable levels to schools in White neighborhoods might apply the criterion that disparities in excess of plus or minus 5% in expenditures per pupil indicate inequality (Berk and Hartman 1972). However, the use of such external baselines by themselves still leaves open the question of causal inference. It may be difficult to determine if the program or some other set of factors produced the observed relationship between outcomes of interest and the external metric. For example, the lower funding of schools in Black neighborhoods may stem from discriminatory policies of the school board or the greater seniority, and, therefore, higher salaries, of teachers working in the schools of White neighborhoods.

Some Research Designs for Estimating Effectiveness

The discussion of comparison group strategies in the last few pages has necessarily been couched in relatively abstract terms.

The actual practice of choosing among such strategies leads to a large variety of research designs. A typology of research design types commonly used for assessing the effectiveness of programs is shown in Table 4.2.

There are two dimensions to the typology: (1) what is known about the mechanism by which some units (e.g., people) were exposed to the program and some units were exposed to the control condition, and (2) how a causal effect may be operationalized. Regarding knowledge of the assignment mechanism (middle column in Table 4.2), there are three possible situations. First, the mechanism may be known, but the result (i.e., assignment to the experimental or control condition) cannot be known in advance. That is, the mechanism is stochastic. The equivalent of a coin flip is an illustration. Second, the mechanism may be known, and it is possible to know the result in advance as well. That is, the mechanism is deterministic. Assigning solely on the basis of some observable characteristic such as income is an illustration; individuals with incomes below some threshold

Table 4.2 A Typology of Research Designs

Research Design Type	Assignment Mechanism	Treatment Effects
I. Randomized ("true") Experiments	Known-Stochastic	$\bar{Y}_E - \bar{Y}_C$
II. Regression-discontinuity	Known-deterministic	$(\bar{Y}_E|A) - (\bar{Y}_C|A)$
III. Interrupted time series	Unknown-hypothesized	$(\bar{Y}_{t2}|T, V) - (\bar{Y}_{t1}|T, V)$
IV. Cross-section	Unknown-hypothesized	$(\bar{Y}_E|X) - (\bar{Y}_C|X)$
V. Polled Cross-Section time series (panel)	Unknown hypothesized	$(\bar{Y}_{E,t2}|T, V, X) - (\bar{Y}_C, \bar{Y}_{E,t1}|T, V, X)$

NOTE: $\bar{Y}$ = "average" outcome; E = experimental group; C = comparison group; A = assigment variable(s); $t1$ = before the intervention; $t2$ = after the intervention; X = confounded variables covariates; T = trends; and V = events.

may be given income subsidies and individuals with income above some threshold may not be given income subsidies. Third, the assignment may be unknown but hypothesized. For example, there may be a number of factors determining which households adopt recycling practices and which do not. It may be impossible to know exactly what those factors are, but it is certainly possible to develop informed hypotheses.

Under the operationalization of causal effects, there are a number of different possibilities. The most important differences, however, depend on whether the causal effect is defined in terms of cross-sectional comparisons or longitudinal comparisons and on what additional information may be taken into account to make the comparison "fair." For example, we will see that for randomized experiments, the usual comparisons are cross-sectional, and fair comparisons require nothing more than knowing what intervention was received by each unit. Other designs are more complicated to analyze. In any case, for each design there are several ways to define a treatment effect (e.g., as a difference or a ratio). Those listed in the last column of Table 4.2 are among the most common and will suffice for expositional purposes.

Design Type I:
Randomized ("True") Experiments

We begin our exposition of Table 4.2 returning to randomized experiments. While we have a few new points to make, our main goal is to provide a benchmark by which alternative designs may be judged. The "gold standard" for internal validity requires random assignment to experimental and control groups.

As we have observed a number of times already, the essential feature of true experiments is the random assignment of the treatment to units and the random withholding of the treatment from units, constituting, respectively, an experimental and a control group. The mechanism by which the assignment occurs is, therefore, known. However, it is a *chance* mechanism, because there is no way of determining before the assignment which units will be experimentals and which will be controls.

The uncertainty creates no problems, however, because, in effect, assignment results from a fair lottery, which on the average makes the units assigned to the experimental group the same as the units assigned to the control group. That is, all external confounding influences are eliminated; the groups are on the average comparable before the intervention is introduced.

True experiments have a number of other assets (Berk et al. 1985). Perhaps most important, appropriate estimates of treatment impact can be obtained from a simple comparison between the "average" outcome for the experimentals and the "average" outcome for the controls. The "simple" comparison may be a difference (as shown in Table 4.2) or a ratio.[9] And the "average" may be a mean, median, or any other sensible measure of central tendency. One might in an experiment on the impact of a job training program, for instance, use the difference in postintervention median income between the experimentals and controls. Another important advantage of randomized experiments is that, typically, the assumptions necessary for statistical inferences are likely to be met.

This is not to say that randomized experiments necessarily lead to straightforward results. Everything depends on the random assignment being implemented as designed. If, for instance, agency personnel override the random assignment, even with the best of intentions, the unique assets of true experiments are at least debased (Berk and Sherman 1988). For example, in an experiment undertaken in Detroit on the deterrent impact of arresting shoplifters, individuals apprehended for shoplifting by department store security personnel were to be assigned at random to one of two conditions: (1) arrest and (2) reprimand and release. However, the assignment pattern was initially alternating: odd cases received arrest and even cases received reprimand and release. As a result, store personnel were often able to anticipate the assignment outcome and some used this information to pair particular individuals with particular treatments. With perhaps the best of intentions, they were trying to make sure that accused shoplifters got "what they deserved."

Still, even if units are actually assigned at random, two additional assumptions must be made (Rubin 1986). First, the subjects must not be affected by the assignment mechanism itself. For example, suppose that, in a job training experiment, individuals who are randomly assigned to the control condition (e.g., job referral assistance only) misinterpret the assignment as an assessment of their potential. That is, they believe, incorrectly, that they were less deserving than individuals assigned to the control group. Then, a resulting reduction in self-confidence may translate into poorer performance in the job market.

Second, one must assume that intervention received by the experimentals has no impact on the controls, and vice versa. For example, suppose one wanted to test the impact of teaching mathematics in a new way to primary school students. If teachers in the control group are threatened by the new technology, they may just work harder within their conventional curriculum to "show" administrators that the new approach is unnecessary. This is sometimes called a "John Henry Effect" and clearly affects treatment content.[10]

If either assumption is substantially violated—that the assignment mechanism does not affect the outcome and that what one group receives does not affect the outcome of the other group—there are at least two complications. Clearly, treatment content has been altered, which makes any substantive interpretations of the results more difficult. In addition, a number of important properties of the data necessary for statistical inference no longer hold. For example, the outcomes for the experimentals and controls may be related (not independent).

In short, like all empirical research, randomized experiments rely on assumptions that are often not directly testable. The number of such assumptions, however, is *far fewer* than other research designs require and can be kept to a minimum if random assignment is properly implemented. One implication is that randomized experiments must be implemented with great care. Another is that straightforward interpretations do not necessarily follow from results of true experiments: caveat emptor.

Design Type II:
Regression Discontinuity
(Assignment by Observed Variables)

Some programs are administered using a clear set of rules for selecting participants. For example, some college fellowship programs allocate fellowships on the basis of scores received on standardized tests (e.g., the National Merit Scholarship Test). In a similar fashion, eligibility for food stamps is determined by income. Likewise, access to privileges in prison is often decided by the number of disciplinary infractions. Note that in all three illustrations there is, at least in principle, a threshold that cleanly and definitively determines whether benefits are provided. Individuals above (or below) the threshold receive benefits, while individuals below (or above) the threshold do not. That is, there is no uncertainty in the assignment process.

If such administrative rules are followed faithfully, it is possible to obtain fair (unbiased) estimates of treatment effect if, in *addition* to the assumptions required for randomized experiments, one additional assumption is met. One must assume some *functional form* for the relationship between the variable used to determine who gets support (e.g., test scores) and the outcome (e.g., grade point average in college). A linear form or simple polynomial is commonly used.

The reason for the additional assumption is easily understood. Recall that, in the case of random assignment, the experimentals and controls were on the average comparable. When assignment is determined by some threshold on an observed variable such as a test score, however, there is good reason to suspect that the experimentals and controls are *not* comparable (and hence "control" group is not really appropriate). Other things being equal, for instance, students with higher test scores may well perform better in college.

The solution is to use information about the relationship between the assignment variable and the outcome to infer how the comparison group would have performed if their values on the assignment variable were on the average the same as those of the experimental group. If, for example, the relationship between test scores and later grade point average is linear, one can easily *extrapolate* what the grade point averages of the comparison group would have been had they had test scores identical on the average to the experimental group. Then, these extrapolated values may be compared to the *observed* grade point averages of the experimentals. For example, one might compute the simple difference between the two. Unfortunately, if the functional form is wrong, the extrapolations will be wrong, and, as a result, the comparison will be misleading. In practice, there is often evidence in the data that may make one functional form more plausible than others. It cannot be overemphasized, however, that there will be *no* experimental and comparison group members with the *same* values on the assignment variable. Consequently, there are no means to verify empirically that the assumed functional form is correct. Evidence for a particular extrapolation is a long way from proof that the extrapolation is accurate.

The argument just made is simply summarized in Table 4.2 in the column "Treatment Effects." If one knows the assignment variable (or combination of variables) and how it was used (i.e., the threshold), one may obtain unbiased estimates of the treatment effect after controlling (via statistical procedures such as analysis of covariance) for the assignment variable. That is, the treatment effect is conditional upon values of the assignment variable ("A"). It is in this process of making statistical adjustments that a functional form must be assumed and one is essentially looking for a discontinuity (or "jump") in the estimated regression line based on that functional form. Hence the term "regression discontinuity design."

The regression discontinuity design is, for some, counterintuitive. It is hard to believe, apparently, that after controlling for the assignment variable (and only the assignment variable) the experimental and comparison groups are on the average comparable. But, the assignment variable is the sole vehicle by which assignment was undertaken, and how it was used is known exactly for each unit. In an analogous manner to random assignment, controlling for the assignment variable, therefore, severs *all* relationships between variables related to the outcome and the intervention assigned. Unbiased estimates follow.

Regression discontinuity designs are particularly useful when programs assign benefits on the basis of some measured variable. With no extra effort, a powerful quasi-experimental design is already in place (e.g., Berk and Rauma 1983). In addition, regression discontinuity designs are sometimes useful alternatives to true experiments when random assignment is politically or ethically unacceptable. One may assign on the basis of "need" or any other attribute as long as there is an observable variable on which a threshold may be placed (for more details see Trochim 1984).

Design Type III:
Interrupted Time Series

Interrupted time series designs are based on repeated measures, over time, of some outcome. Simply put, the idea is to compare the time trend before an intervention with the time trend after. For example, a downward trend in the conviction rate for a particular jurisdiction may be reversed after more prosecutors are hired. Or air pollution levels downwind from a major power plant may be relatively stable over several years until a dramatic drop materializes following the introduction of cleaner-burning fuels.

Time series analyses are especially important for estimating the net impacts of full coverage programs. Under full coverage, all the units that could be served are being served. Consequently, there are no reasonable comparison groups. However, if a relatively large number of observations are collected before and after the intervention, the earlier period provides a comparison "group" for the later period. Thus it may be possible to study the effect of the enactment of a gun control law in a particular jurisdiction, but only if the evaluator has access to a sufficiently lengthy series of crime statistics for gun-related offenses, both before and after the law was enacted. Or the effects of changing pricing policies on residential water consumption can be studied by analyzing the consumption trends, if consumption data can be found before and after the pricing policy changes (Berk et al. 1981). Of course, for many interventions such long-term measures do not exist. For example, there are no long-term, detailed time series on the incidence of certain acute diseases, making it difficult to assess the impact on those diseases of medicare or medicaid.

The basic logic underlying the analysis or interrupted time series designs is quite simple. The time series before the intervention is analyzed so that temporal trends (or "patterns" more generally) before the intervention are characterized as accurately as possible. For example, the number of burglaries may be increasing at an increasing rate. Then, the preintervention trends are used to *project* what would have happened without the intervention. Finally, the observed trends after the intervention are compared with the projections.[11] In its simplest form the preintervention mean is compared to the postintervention mean, as shown in Table 4.2 (where "T" stands for trends and "V" stands for events).

While capturing the preintervention trends is a necessary condition for accurate estimates of treatment impact,[12] it is not sufficient. One must also take into account events, in addition to the intervention, that are related to *when* the intervention was introduced and could affect postintervention trends. For example, a reduction in water consumption after an increase in the marginal price might be obscured by an overall increase in water consumption because of a major leak in the water distribution system. Or an apparent reduction in water consumption after an increase in the marginal price may really result from the installation of new water-saving irrigation technology that was purchased well before the price increase was even contemplated. In other words, one must take into account events whose effects may be confounded with the intervention. The key idea is that events occurring about the same *time* as the intervention must be addressed.

Put in the terms we used above, the "assignment" process is

one of timing. All units receive the intervention because there is only one unit: a company, a household, a city, a school district, or even a single individual (Kadzin 1982). What needs to be addressed is not which units receive the intervention and which do not, but *when* the intervention is introduced. It is this assignment process that must be considered, and all variables related to the *timing* of the intervention, that also may affect the postintervention trends, must be taken into account. We show this in Table 4.2 by including as "conditioning variables" not only time trends ("T") but confounding events ("V"). In practice, the Vs are "taken into account" with multivariate statistical techniques that are beyond the scope of this book.[13]

The most serious limitation on time series designs is the need to properly adjust, in the statistical analysis, for preexisting trends ("Ts") and events that are roughly contemporaneous with the intervention ("Vs"). These trends cannot be known with the same confidence that the assignment mechanism can be known for either the randomized experiment or the regression discontinuity design. They must be hypothesized, capitalizing on social science theory, past research, and information in the data on hand. And there is ultimately no way to directly test whether the Ts and Vs taken into account are the full set of Ts and Vs that should have been taken into account. Put another way, *in addition* to all of the assumptions required for randomized experiments, one must accurately hypothesize what Ts and Vs are relevant and, typically, the functional form of their relationships with the outcome.

Another obstacle is that the number of preintervention and postintervention observations must be sufficient to reveal accurately preintervention and postintervention time trends (more than 25 observations for each are sometimes recommended). For this reason, interrupted time series designs are often restricted to outcomes for which governmental or other groups routinely collect and publish the needed statistics. Despite these and other drawbacks, however, the interrupted time series design can be very effective when more powerful designs are not available.

Design Type IV:
Cross-Sectional Designs

Whereas interrupted time series designs were characterized by temporal variation only, cross-sectional designs are characterized by cross-sectional variation only. One is simply examining whether two or more sets of units differ at some specific moment in time. One set, for example, might be cities that earlier passed rent control ordinances and another set might be cities that did not. Then the central empirical comparison might be between the current median vacancy rate for similar kinds of apartments in the two kinds of cities: the median vacancy rate for rent controlled cities versus the median vacancy rate for nonrent control cities. That is, the *outcome* is measured at only one moment in time and only as a posttest. Hence, comparisons can only be between units at that historical moment.

Much as in randomized experiments and regression discontinuity designs, one is interested in a comparison of units exposed to the intervention with units not exposed to the intervention. However, unlike true experiments and regression discontinuity designs, the assignment mechanism must be hypothesized. And if the hypothesized assignment mechanism is not effectively the same as the true assignment mechanism, the comparisons between the exposed and unexposed units will lead to misleading treatment effect estimates.

Stated a bit differently, the problem is that members of the exposed and unexposed groups are not likely to be on the average comparable before the intervention is introduced. Insofar as these differences are *also* related to the outcome measure, the effect of preexisting differences between the experimental and comparison groups will be confounded with the treatment effect. The only hope, then, is to make the groups *conditionally* comparable by controlling for the variables determining assignment. We show this in Table 4.2 by making the treatment effect conditional on "X."

Consider, for example, an ongoing program in the San Francisco area to make judges more sensitive to the special nature of domestic violence cases. Judges are offered weekend workshops in which they learn about the nature of domestic violence and the special needs of both victims and offenders. As a result of these workshops, sentencing patterns are supposed to change. Now, suppose that the potential change in sentencing patterns is being estimated by comparing the sentences given by judges who participate in the workshops with the sentences given by judges who do not (i.e., a cross-sectional comparison).

For expositional purposes, assume that judges were simply encouraged to volunteer for the weekend workshops.[14] Clearly, not all judges in the state would participate, and those who did might well differ from those who did not. For example, judges already concerned about the issues might well be the ones more likely to volunteer. And these judges might *already* sentence differently. Alternatively, they might be individuals who would have changed their sentencing practices *anyway* in the near future. How then can a fair comparison be made?

For simplicity, suppose that "concern about domestic violence" was the only factor affecting the likelihood that judges would volunteer for the workshops. Clearly, if for each experimental group judge a comparison group judge could be found who was equally "concerned," the two groups would be matched on the "selection" variable on which participation depended. The two groups would then be comparable person by person. For reasons briefly mentioned earlier, exact matching is often impractical and, as an alternative, statistical adjustments are often undertaken that equate the experimental and comparison groups on the average. That is, the central tendencies (usually means) of the two groups are equated on factors that differ *before* the intervention is introduced; the two groups are made comparable on the average. In this illustration, the group of the judges who did not volunteer would have the same *average* level of "concern about domestic violence" as the group judges who did. With these adjustments made, the groups can be fairly compared.

In practice, the necessary adjustments are not easily made. *In addition* to all of the assumptions required in randomized experiments, one must assume that *all* of the variables affecting assignment and the outcome are known and measured.[15] These variables should be chosen by developing a "selection model" for how units are assigned to the experimental and comparison conditions. But because such a model is only hypothesized, internal validity is always in jeopardy. That is, there is no direct way to empirically validate the hypothesized selection model.

Design Type V:
Pooled Cross-Sectional and
Time Series Designs (Panels)

Randomized experiments and regression discontinuity designs may rely on cross-sectional (across units) and time series (over time) information. Cross-sectional comparisons are made between individuals who are exposed to the intervention and those who are not. In addition, statistical power may be improved by including measures of the outcome variable *before* the intervention. That is, while preintervention measures of the outcome variable are often not needed for unbiased treatment effect estimates, "pretest" measures allow one to more easily separate "real" treatment effects from "noise."[16] Thus true experiments and regression discontinuity designs may capitalize on longitudinal comparisons.

Under pooled cross-sectional and time series designs (also known as "panel" designs), both cross-sectional and longitudinal comparisons may be made. However, we only include those situations in which the assignment mechanism is unknown. That is, just as in interrupted time series and cross-sectional designs, the assignment mechanism must be hypothesized.

Consider, for example, whether a new drug slows the "conversion" to AIDS among those people infected with the AIDS retrovirus (HIV). The drug is made available to physicians to prescribe as they see fit with the constraint that only one prescription for a week of treatment is permitted per patient. Now, imagine a research design in which monthly data are collected for several years on a sample of HIV-infected individuals. That is, there is a monthly time series for each individual. Assume that the outcome measure is the "T-cell count"; the lower the count, the more compromised the immune system. The drug is the intervention. For those who take the new drug, the prescription's date is recorded. In addition, information is collected on a number of physical and behavioral variables potentially related to *both* the taking of the drug and the conversion to AIDS: other drugs being taken, other illnesses, sexual behavior, the use of "recreational drugs," diet, exercise, and the like. For example, an infected individual who feels he is eating well and getting sufficient exercise may be less likely to see a physician and also less likely to "convert." Or an infected individual who engages in "high-risk behavior," such as intravenous drug use, may be more likely to see a physician (as a precaution) and more likely to "convert."

The analysis of the drug data may be initially seen as a set of interrupted time series analyses, one for each individual who took the new drug. As before, one can compare time trends before taking the drug with time trends after, and potentially confounding events, such as contracting another illness, would need to be taken into account. Just as in an interrupted time series design, the simplest analysis would contrast the mean (or median) T-cell count before the intervention with the mean (or median) T-cell count after the intervention.

In addition, however, comparisons can be made across individuals between those who took the new drug and those who did not, much as in purely cross-sectional designs. And just as in purely cross-sectional designs, all variables affecting treatment assignment (i.e., taking the new drug) and the outcome (i.e., T-cell count) would need to be known, measured, and used in any analysis of the data. In the simplest analysis, the conditional mean for the individuals who took the drug would be compared with the conditional mean for the individuals who did not take the drug.

But, it is possible to do better than either the longitudinal or cross-sectional analyses alone. One can effectively combine the two to address both confounding temporal variables and confounding cross-sectional variables. Again focusing on perhaps the simplest analysis, the mean T-cell count for the "nontreated" individuals would include the T-cell counts for individuals who were not treated at all and the T-cell counts during the preintervention period for individuals who ultimately were treated. The mean T-cell count for the "treated" individuals would include the T-cell counts for people who took the new drug in the postintervention period. And both means would be adjusted for (i.e., would be conditional upon) trends ("T"), roughly contemporaneous events ("V"), and assignment variables ("X"). That is, one would adjust for both temporal and cross-sectional confounders.

Because pooled cross-sectional and time series designs typically involve more data collection than either cross-sectional or interrupted time designs alone, one might wonder when they are worth the effort. In general, they should be undertaken when resources allow, assuming that true experiments and regression discontinuity designs are not practical. First, thought of as many interrupted time series, the prospects for external validity are better than for a single interrupted time series. In our AIDS example, it is possible to explore how well the drug works for a large group of people, some of whom presumably vary in important ways. Second, thought of as a set of cross-sectional comparisons arrayed over time, the prospects for external validity are better than for a single-point-in-time cross-sectional comparison. Again using our AIDS example, it is possible to explore how effective the drug is depending on when in the progression of the illness it is taken. Finally, the longitudinal and cross-sectional variation allow for both longitudinal and cross-sectional threats to internal validity to be addressed, at least in principle. In the AIDS illustration, one can adjust, for example, for time trends in the T-cell count (e.g., cycles during a downward trend), the confounding effect of earlier illnesses (e.g., herpes), and the confounding effect of age differences across infected individuals.

Stage 7:
Was the Program Worth It?

The Cost-Effectiveness Question

In the previous chapter, the issue of cost-effectiveness was addressed. We have little to add here because the issues for new programs and ongoing programs are much the same. Perhaps the major difference is that for ongoing programs, there is often more information about the long term to take into account. For example, insofar as staff salaries are tied to seniority, ongoing programs may become more expensive in constant dollars as their staffs age. For a new program, there is very little information about these kinds of processes that unfold over the long haul. In a similar fashion, there will be more information about benefits. The long term returns to job training, for example, may be estimable from data rather than hypothesized from theory or extrapolated from past research. Given the central role of discounting, having data on such long terms costs and benefits can be very useful.

Notes

1. We say "even" because physical outcomes are supposed to be more easily conceptualized and measured than behavioral outcomes.
2. This can happen even if the definition of success is clearly stated in advance. However, when there is clear and explicit agreement among key actors about how good is good enough, there will more likely be one "official" interpretation of the results. Moreover, a clear definition of success before the data are analyzed lends additional credibility to the results. It is harder to argue that someone "made" the results come out in a particular way. Ideally, central stakeholders should settle on how success (or failure) will be defined and then let the research process independently unfold.
3. It is important to keep in mind that the concepts being illustrated are generally applicable; for example, in the adult population, one can distinguish individuals, households, neighborhoods and cities for different levels of aggregation and life cycle stages for the time periods of adult life.
4. We use the term "comparison group" as a general term to be distinguished from "control group." Control groups are comparison groups that have been constructed by random assignment.
5. The definition of a confounding variable requires that it be related to both the assignment of treatment and control conditions (which it was in this case) and the outcome (which it may not have been in this case).
6. Because classes are being randomized, not students, it is necessary to have a relatively large number of classes randomly allocated to the experimental and control conditions to be assured that the two sets of classrooms are approximately equivalent before the treatment is applied.
7. Structural equation models are statistical techniques for representing in mathematical form one's theory about how an outcome is produced. The equation for a straight line taught in elementary algebra $(y = mx + b)$ is an

illustration of a very simple structural equation and would be appropriate if, in part, the treatment (x) affected the outcome (y) in a linear fashion. The relevant data would include observations for x (e.g., memberships in the treatment or control groups) and y (e.g., earnings). Statistical procedures would be used to estimate the values of the two parameters, m and b. The slope of the line is represented by m, and it is the estimate of program impact. In the absence of random assignment, structural equation models are far more complicated and controversial. A latent variable is a variable that is not directly measured. Rather, "indicators" of the latent variable are measured. For example, an indicator of the amount of crime in a neighborhood (a latent variable) may be the number of reported crimes.

8. Matching is an underutilized technique in evaluation research. No doubt, its lack of popularity stems from a belief that matching is only practical for very large samples (e.g., 25,000 cases). Suppose, for example, that for every experimental group member who is White, unmarried, unemployed, female, with two children under three, one must find a comparison group member who has exactly the same configuration of characteristics. And suppose that one must find a match for every member of the experimental group. Quite likely, a very large number of individuals would have to be screened for all of the necessary matches to be found. However, with new developments such as "nearest neighbor matching," matches can be approximate and not literally identical. Nearly the same levels of internal validity is achieved but with far less searching. Hence, far smaller samples can be used (Rosenbaum and Rubin 1985).

9. We are not considering here the possibility of "interaction effects" in which the treatment has more impact for some units than others. For example, an arrest may deter first-time wife beaters but not individuals with a long history of spousal violence. While interaction effects are common and very important for policy purposes, they are beyond the scope of this book. They are considered, however, in a number of standard references (e.g., Rossi and Freeman 1985).

10. One way to prevent such problems is to "blind" subjects to interventions they receive. This is common in clinical trials in which the control group receives a "*placebo*" that, to the experiment's subjects, is indistinguishable from the "real" treatment; neither the experimentals nor the controls know what group they are in. For example, both groups may be asked to drink a milky liquid twice a day that looks and tastes the same whether or not the experimental medicine is included. There are closely related issues in how the outcome is measured. In particular, it is important to prevent knowledge of the intervention received to affect how the outcome is *recorded*. For example, it is common in clinical trials to prevent physicians who will be diagnosing the outcome illness (e.g., cancer) from knowing whether patients are members of the experimental or the control group. Physicians who know which patients are members of the experimental group, for instance, may be inadvertently inclined to see improvements when there really is none. When the experimental subjects do not know whether they are experimentals or controls, the study is called a "*single blind*" experiment. When the individuals doing the measuring are also in the dark, the study is called a "*double blind*" experiment.

11. Actually, what is done is to remove ("residualize" or "filter") the preexisting trends so that comparisons between the preintervention and postintervention can be fairly made.

12. The preintervention trends may be captured by observable patterns in the preintervention time series (e.g., a linear increase over time) or by variables explaining the trend. For example, increases in water consumption may be a function of population increases. Insofar as population has been measured over the preintervention period, it can be used to model trends in consumption.

13. One can construct a randomized experiment within an interrupted time series framework by randomly assigning *when* the treatment is introduced (Edgington 1987; chap. 10). These are a special type of "single subject design."

14. As this is being written, a randomized experiment is actually the design anticipated. Among a set of judges who volunteer for the workshops, a random half will have their workshops postponed six months. During those six months, the first set of judges is a legitimate experimental group and the second set of judges is a legitimate control group. And it is the sentencing patterns for the two groups over those six months from which treatment effects will be estimated.

15. The good news is that *only* variables related to the assignment and the outcome need be included. Variables affecting only the assignment *or* only the outcome need not be included to obtain unbiased estimates.

16. Sometimes pretest measures are necessary control variables. The sentence given to a convicted felon may depend on the length of an earlier sentence; the earlier sentence is a pretest measure for the sentencing outcome. Also, sometimes pretest measures can be used to control for unobserved differences between units (sometimes called "unobserved heterogeneity").

Some Final Observations

The field of evaluation research is scarcely out of its infancy as a social scientific activity. The first large-scale field experiments were initiated in the mid-1960s. Concern for large-scale national evaluations of social programs had their origins in the War on Poverty. The art of designing large-scale implementation and monitoring studies is still evolving rapidly. Concern with the scientific validity of qualitative research has just begun. As part of all this, the demand for sound program evaluations continues to grow.

In this context, perhaps the best overall message is to keep evaluations as simple as possible. Simple programs will typically be hard enough to design and field. Simple research designs usually will be sufficiently demanding. And simple data analyses will likely tax the best evaluators available. Put another way, there is no such thing as a routine evaluation. Adding unnecessary complexity to the burden is to turn a promising opportunity into almost certain disaster.

Simplicity, however, is not enough. It is also important to think defensively as if Murphy's Law always applied. Evaluation research is often a mine field of day-to-day problems for which the proper preparation can make an enormous difference. For example, it is typically useful to get, in writing, all significant understandings between the evaluator and program administrators (e.g., the definition of a successful outcome). Even under the best of circumstances and with the best of intentions, organizational memories can be very short. Likewise, it is essential that quality control procedures be introduced for all facets of data collection: sampling, measurement, data entry, and the like. Indeed, it is often prudent to allocate as much as 20 percent of one's evaluation research budget to data quality control. And, before diving into a fancy statistical analysis, it is essential to carefully inspect the data for errors of various sorts that will almost certainly be present. This means not just a search for isolated "outliers," but internal consistency checks for anomalous relationships among key variables.

Finally, there is no recipe. Prescriptions for "successful" evaluations are, in practice, prescriptions for failure. The techniques that evaluators may bring to bear are only tools, and even the very best of tools do not ensure a worthy product. Just as for any craft, there is no substitute for intelligence, experience, perseverence, and a touch of whimsy.

Appendix

Guide to Literature on, Professional Associations of, and Organizations Engaged in Evaluation Research and Social Policy Research in the United States

"The complete policy researcher" must be a knowledgeable methodologist, a creative theoretician, a capable manager, and a skilled politician. This is not the job description for a graduate student who is never quite able to understand what internal validity is all about, whose conception of theory is limited to a terminological maze that makes no claims about how things "work", and whose administrative skills are taxed by managing to get a dissertation typed and turned in on time. Herbert L. Costner, "Commentaries" in Demerath, Larsen, and Schuessler, eds., *Social Policy and Sociology*, (New York: Academic Press, 1975, p. 262)

I. Some General References

The books and journals devoted largely to evaluation research methods and to evaluation studies have increased considerably in the past decade. Listed below are some of the major general references of which you should be aware if you want to become knowledgeable about evaluation

101

research theory and practice. The commentaries after each reference may be used as a guide to content.

A. Evaluation Journals

Evaluation Review: A Journal of Applied Social Research. (Formerly *Evaluation Quarterly.*) Regarded as the best of the professional journals. Biased toward quantitative and formal approaches. Published bimonthly by Sage Publications. Interdisciplinary, often technical, and always of high quality.

Evaluation News. An official publication of the American Evaluation Association, formerly published by the Evaluation Network (see organizations, below). Published quarterly by Sage. Contains mainly short articles primarily addressed to professional issues and to substantive evaluation problems. Contains a useful set of short reviews of new publications in evaluation. Tends to favor more qualitative evaluation styles.

New Directions for Program Evaluation. Quarterly journal of the American Evaluation Association (formerly the Evaluation Research Society) published by Jossey-Bass. Mainly special issues, some based on annual meetings of the society.

Evaluation and Program Planning. Independent quarterly specializing in evaluations of human services programs, especially mental health programs. Now officially the journal of the Eastern Evaluation Research Society, a regional affiliate of the American Evaluation Association.

Evaluation Studies Review Annual. Annual collection of the "best" articles and unpublished pieces on evaluation methods and findings. Published by Sage and edited by editors separately picked for each annual. Quality variable but some issues are extremely good.

Policy Analysis. Quarterly published by the University of California Press and edited by Berkeley's Public Policy School. Largely devoted to policy analysis although there are many articles on evaluations.

Journal of Policy Analysis and Management. Published quarterly by John Wiley and edited at Harvard's Kennedy School, this is probably the best policy analysis journal going. Contains good reviews of recent literature.

B. Sometime Evaluation Journals

These are journals in which evaluations and related policy research issues often appear, but not consistently.

Human Organization. Journal of the Society for Applied Anthropology.

Social Problems. Journal of the Society for the Scientific Study of Social Problems.

Journal of Social Issues. Journal of the Society for the Psychological Study of Social Problems (an affiliate of the APA).

Journal of Applied Psychology. Although heavy on industrial psychology, occasional articles on evaluation appear.

Journal of Human Resources. Devoted largely to issues in labor economics and training.

Medical Anthropology. Devoted to cultural anthropology studies of medical problems and medical care.

Health and Human Behavior. Published by the American Sociological Association, occasionally containing evaluation studies.

Social Science Research. Contains many articles on evaluation issues and studies.

American Journal of Public Health. Journal of the American Public Health Association, routinely contains evaluations of health services organizations.

In addition, from time to time, the mainline professional journals will publish articles on evaluation, especially on epistemological and technical issues.

C. Major General References On Evaluation
Note: Especially important references are
marked with * *.

Bennett, A. and A. Lumsdaine. 1975. *Evaluations and Experiments.* Academic Press.

Excellent (although a little old) compilation of papers on field experiments evaluating innovative programs.

Campbell, D. T. and J. Stanley. 1967. *Experimental and Quasi-Experimental Designs for Research*. Rand McNally.

A classic that has dominated the evaluation research design literature since publication. Concerned primarily with educational evaluations but very general.

**Cronbach, L. J. 1982. *Designing Evaluations of Educational and Social Programs*. Jossey-Bass.

An excellent text advancing a counter-Campbellian perspective that makes a great deal of sense.

**Cook, T. and D. T. Campbell. 1979. *Quasi-Experimentation*. Rand McNally.

Excellent exposition of research designs used commonly in evaluations by two of the best practitioners of the art of exposition. Somewhat removed from practice, however.

Cronbach, L. J. (and associates). 1980. *Toward Reform of Program Evaluation*. Jossey-Bass.

A founding father of the field and a large cast of associates at Stanford ruminate over the faults of program evaluation and suggest reforms in the form of 95 "theses." Sensible suggestions although ponderously written.

Franklin, J. L. and J. H. Thrasher. 1976. *An Introduction to Program Evaluation*. John Wiley.

An elementary introduction to program evaluation in the public health and health delivery fields.

Guba, E. and Y. Lincoln. 1982. *Effective Evaluation*. Jossey-Bass.

Advocates of naturalistic, responsive evaluations. Perhaps the best case made for qualitative approaches to evaluation.

Guttentag, M. and E. Struening, eds. 1975. *Handbook of Evaluation Research*. 2 vols. Sage.

Although very much out of date, these two volumes are quite comprehensive in their coverage of major issues and substantive applications. Most of the chapter contributions (by quite well-known authors) were written in the late 1960s—just as the field began to flower.

House, E. R. 1982. *Evaluating with Validity*. Sage.

Long essay on evaluations that can be used to improve programs, especially educational ones. Takes an anti-social-science viewpoint.

Judd, C. M. and D. S. Kenny. 1981. *Estimating the Effects of Social Interventions*. Cambridge University Press.

A useful, if somewhat dated, survey of approaches to the quantitative assessment and estimation of net impacts of social programs.

Morris, L. L., ed. 1988. *Program Evaluation Kit. 2nd ed., 8 vols. Sage.*

A set of cookbooks written to help local agencies carry out evaluation studies; mainly oriented toward local educational agencies. Simply written and quite good, but not very sophisticated technically. Do not use on evaluations that count.

Patton, M. 1980. *Qualitative Evaluation Methods*. Sage.

Strong advocacy of qualitative approaches, but not the best reasoned.

Riecken, H. and R. Boruch, and associates. 1974. *Social Experimentation*. Academic Press.

Outcome of an SSRC committee on social experimentation. Excellent and simply written review of the major issues (as understood in the early 1970s) in the design and conduct of large-scale social experiments.

**Rossi, P. H. and H. Freeman. 1985. *Evaluation: A Systematic Approach*. 4th ed. Sage.

An excellent introduction to evaluation research, sprinkled throughout with many examples. Probably the best text around for beginners; well written.

Rossi, P. H. and W. Williams. 1974. *Evaluating Social Programs*. Academic Press.

Outgrowth of a 1969 conference on evaluation. Excellent papers but out of date. Should be read out of antiquarian interest.

Scriven, Michael. 1980. *Evaluation Thesaurus*. 3rd ed. Scarecrow. (private press owned by Scriven).

Scriven's views on evaluation given in the guise of a dictionary of evaluation terms. Written with grace and skill.

Scriven, M. 1980. *The Logic of Evaluation*. Scarecrow.

An eccentric but very literate and amusing review of evaluation as an enterprise that must bend to fit the needs of the program being evaluated.

Suchman, E. A. 1967. *Evaluation Research*. Russell Sage.

Old but very good. The best of the early comprehensive reviews of the field. Mainly addressed to the public health field.

Wholey, J. S. 1979. *Evaluation: Promise and Performance*. Urban Institute.

Heavy emphases on program monitoring and evaluability assessments, especially of established programs; can also be regarded as a do-it-yourself advocate.

NOTE: A few publishing houses—Sage, Jossey-Bass, and Academic Press—dominate the publication of evaluation-oriented books and texts. See their catalogues for long lists of general references in the field.

D. Some Major Technical Reference Journals

Journal of the American Statistical Association (JASA).   An excellent diverse journal that contains an "applications" section that is especially of interest to evaluators and applied social scientists. Articles are often quite difficult.

Journal of the Royal Statistical Society. The British counterpart of JASA and very similar in content and style, but in three separate series.

Econometrica. Journal of the Econometrics Society; publishes articles on statistical issues, substantive problems, and economic theory. Useful (and often difficult) for the model-building side of evaluation research.

Journal of Econometrics. Much like *Econometrica.*

Psychometrika. Journal of the Psychometric Society; focuses on measurement issues and the analysis of observational data. Often quite difficult.

Biometrika. Journal of the Biometric Society, publishing articles on statistical issues in the biological and health sciences. Often contains interesting articles on true experiments and approximations of them, but often quite difficult.

Biometrics. Much like *Biometrika.*

Technometrics. Journal of the American Society for Quality Control; publishes articles on statistical applications in the physical, chemical, and engineering fields. Has a lot of good materials for social scientists, especially on research design. Often very difficult.

Journal of Educational Statistics. Publishes articles on statistical applications in educational research. Usually more accessible than the blank-metrics journals.

Sociological Methodology. At one time published by the American Sociological Association, an annual volume of solicited and contributed pieces on methodological issues in sociological research. Uneven in quality and relevance to evaluation. Didactic and review articles are often quite good.

Sociological Methods and Research. Quarterly devoted to sociological research issues. Currently struggling to fill each issue and, as a result, quality is often marginal. There are, however, always some articles relevant to evaluation research.

E. Some General Technical References

These are books that contain expositions of the statistical techniques and research designs used in evaluation research. Usually these also contain discussions of other procedures as well.

Achen, Christopher. 1986. *The Statistical Analysis of Quasi-Experiments*. University of California.

An excellent discussion of what are the appropriate statistical methods to apply to quasi-experiments. Read only in an optimistic mood.

Belsey, David A. et al. 1980. *Regression Diagnostics: Identifying Influential Data and Sources of Collinearity*. John Wiley.

An excellent discussion of some important things that can go wrong in multivariate analyses and some of the things you can do about it (sometimes).

Box George E. P. and Gwilym M. Jenkins. 1976. *Time Series Analysis Forecasting and Control*. Rev. ed. Holden-Day.

The granddaddy reference on modeling time series and still good.

Box, George E. P. et al. 1978. *Statistics for Experimenters*. John Wiley.

An integrated discussion of randomized experiments and analysis of variance in a very accessible form.

Chiang, A. C. 1974. *Fundamental Methods of Mathematical Economics*. McGraw-Hill.

An accessible and excellent reference for applied mathematics (e.g., calculus, matrix algebra) in the social sciences.

Cochran, William G. 1977. *Sampling Techniques*. 3rd ed. John Wiley.

The classic text revised and still excellent, containing sampling theory.

Cochran, William G. 1983. *Planning and Evaluation of Observational Studies*. John Wiley.

Excellent discussion of nonexperimental research procedures.

Cox, D. R. 1958. *Planning Experiments*. John Wiley.

Still an excellent treatment of randomized experiments.

Dillman, Don A. 1978. *Mail and Telephone Surveys: The Total Design Method*. John Wiley.

A real cookbook for the conduct of mail and telephone surveys that get very high response rates. Especially good on mail surveys.

Efron, Bradley. 1982. *The Jackknife, the Bootstrap and Other Resampling Plans*. Society for Industrial and Applied Mathematics.

Still the best overall treatment of resampling procedures, but pithy and a bit dated.

Freedman, David A. et al. 1978. *Statistics*. Norton.
Many argue that this is the best introduction to applied statistics around. Even seasoned researchers find it instructive. Very accessible. New edition due in 1990.

Glass, G. V. et al. 1981. *Meta-Analysis in Social Research*. Sage.
Exposition of methods for aggregating and assessing the results of many evaluations.

Granger, C.W.J. 1980. *Forecasting in Business and Economics*. Academic Press.
A wonderful and accessible introduction to forecasting.

Granger, C.W.J. and P. Newbold. 1986. *Forecasting Economic Time Series*. 2nd ed. Academic Press.
An excellent but relatively advanced treatment of forecasting with good material on intervention analysis. New edition due in 1990.

Groves, Robert M. and R. L. Kahn. 1980. *Surveys by Telephone*. Academic Press.
Excellent discussion of random-digit-dialing methods of telephone surveys and their advantages, by two SRC survey experts.

Hanushek, E. A. and J. E. Jackson. 1978. *Statistical Methods for Social Scientists*. Academic Press.
A very good intermediate econometrics text with lots of examples from sociology and political science. Written for noneconomists.

Harvey, A. C. 1981. *The Econometric Analysis of Time Series*. Halsted.
Probably the best text on the analysis of time series from an econometric point of view.

Hoaglin, David C. et al. 1982. *Data for Decisions*. Abt Books.
A good introduction to how data should be used to make policy decisions. Very accessible.

Hsiao, C. 1986. *Analysis of Panel Data*. Cambridge University Press.
Probably the most recent and thorough treatment of the analysis of panel designs, but not easy going.

Judge, George G. et al. 1985. *The Theory and Practice of Econometrics*. John Wiley.
Perhaps the most wide ranging of the current econometrics texts. Many topics covered and covered well.

Kazdin, A. E. 1982. *Single Case Research Designs: Methods for Clinical and Applied Settings*. Oxford University Press.
Innovative attempt to quantify the study of single cases, mainly in clinical settings.

Kish, Leslie. 1965. *Survey Sampling*. John Wiley.
An old, somewhat out-of-date, but excellent advanced text on the sampling of human populations.

Kish, Leslie. 1987. *Statistical Designs for Research*. John Wiley.
Excellent discussions (although uneven) of experimental and quasi-experimental designs.

Lawless, Jerald F. 1982. *Statistical Models for Lifetime Data*. John Wiley.
Everything you wanted to know about "life history" data and how to handle them, from the biomedical tradition in which "survival analysis" was invented.

Light, Richard J. and D. B. Pillemer. 1984. *Summing Up: The Science of Reviewing Research*. Harvard University Press.
An excellent exposition of how to avoid biases in summarizing the results of many studies.

Little, R.J.A. and D. B. Rubin. 1987. *Statistical Analysis with Missing Data*. John Wiley.
An excellent and current treatment of missing data problems, but fairly difficult and sometimes promising more than it delivers. Except for relatively simple cases, there is no real fix for missing data.

Maddala, G. S. 1983. *Limited-Dependent and Qualitative Variables in Econometrics*. Cambridge University Press.
An excellent but demanding treatment of how to handle "unfriendly" dependent variables. Getting slightly dated, but still very useful.

McCullagh, P. and J. A. Nelder. 1983. *Generalized Linear Models*. Chapman and Hall.
An excellent treatment of an overarching framework in which most statistical procedures used in evaluation research can be placed. Somewhat demanding but worth the effort.

Miles, Mathew and A. Michael Huberman. 1984. *Qualitative Data Analysis*. Sage.
An interesting discussion of how to treat qualitative data derived from "fieldwork" in a rigorous way. Examples used are largely qualitative evaluations.

Mishan, E. J. 1976. *Cost-Benefit Analysis*. 2nd ed. Praeger.
The full treatment; very difficult without some background in economics.

Mosteller, Frederick et al. 1983. *Beginning Statistics with Data Analysis*. Addison-Wesley.
An excellent introductory statistics book with large sections devoted to newer descriptive techniques. Also favors a "robust" (i.e., cautious) view of statistics.

Morrison, D. 1976. *Multivariate Statistical Methods*. 2nd ed. McGraw-Hill.
An excellent intermediate text on multivariate statistical methods popular in education and psychology.

Pindyck, R. S. and D. L. Rubinfeld. 1981. *Econometric Models and Economic Forecast*. 2nd ed. McGraw-Hill.
Perhaps the best intermediate text in econometrics with excellent treatments of simulations and univariate Box-Jenkins procedures.

Pollard, W. E. 1986. *Bayesian Statistics for Evaluation Research: An Introduction*. Sage.
If Bayesian statistics is the wave of the future, this is a good first board to ride.

Rossi, P. H., J. D. Wright, and A. B. Anderson, eds. 1983. *Handbook of Survey Research*. Academic Press.
A good collection of fairly technical papers on sampling, survey questionnaire writing, measurement, and analysis problems in sample surveys; not for the beginner, however.

Rousseeuw, P. J. and A. M. Leroy. 1987. *Robust Regression & Outlier Detection*. John Wiley.
An excellent and accessible treatment of robust regression, including the very newest techniques. Can be purchased with user-friendly software that does many of the techniques described.

Sudman, Seymour. 1976. *Applied Sampling*. Academic Press.
An excellent introduction to population sampling from a practical perspective. (Not for persons looking for sampling theory.)

Sudman, Seymour and Norman M. Bradburn. 1982. *Asking Questions: A Practical Guide to Questionnaire Design*. Jossey-Bass.
Just what the title says it is. The best cookbook yet with plenty of examples.

Thompson, M. S. 1980. *Benefit Cost Analysis for Program Evaluation*. Sage.
A very accessible introduction to cost-benefit analysis used in evaluation of programs.

II. ORGANIZATION OF THE DISCIPLINE

A. Professional Societies (and subsocieties)

American Evaluation Association. An amalgam of the Evaluation Research Society and the Evaluation Network formed in 1985. See entries below for further information on its constituent parts. Everything below that applies to ERS or EN now applies to AEA.

Evaluation Research Society. Annual meeting in October or November. Publishes *New Directions in Evaluation* (quarterly, see above) plus sponsors monographs. Composed primarily of psychologists and sociologists and heavily oriented to human service social programs. Annual meetings are interesting serious, and small enough to enjoy. Membership about 2,000–3,000.

Evaluation Network. Smaller association of evaluators primarily interested in qualitative evaluations of small-scale programs in education and human services.

In addition, sections of the American Psychological Association, American Sociological Association, the American Economic Association, and the American Educational Research Association all have sessions at their annual meetings devoted to problems of evaluation.

B. Major Evaluation Research Producers

Evaluation research is now an industry with university departments, university research organizations, private firms with research branches, and private firms devoted mainly to evaluation, all producing evaluation research. In addition, some evaluation (perhaps a large proportion of all evaluations) is done within agencies with responsibilities for operating social programs.

However, as in other industries, there is considerable concentration. Although perhaps as many as 1,000–2,000 entities do evaluation research, as much as 50% of all the funds are obtained by the top 10–15 largest private firms, who do most of the large-scale (and expensive) evaluations. Some of the largest firms have more social science PhDs on their payrolls than most social science divisions within universities. For example, at its peak in the 1970s, Abt Associates had a staff of more than 100 PhDs and a support staff of about 400 research assistants and clerks.

Some of the largest firms are listed below:

Abt Associates, Inc., Cambridge, MA
The Rand Corporation, Santa Monica, CA (not for profit)
Educational Testing Service, Princeton, NJ (not for profit)
Mathematica, Inc., Princeton, NJ
Battelle Memorial Institute, Columbus, OH (not for profit)
The Urban Institute, Washington DC (not for profit)
The Mitre Corporation, McLean, VA
Westat, Inc., Silver Springs, MD
Research Triangle Institute, Raleigh-Durham, NC (not for profit)

National Analysts, Philadelphia, PA
American Institutes of Research, Pittsburgh, PA

A few of the major university-affiliated research organizations
that are also in the "big" league follow:
Institute for Research on Poverty, University of Wisconsin
NORC (National Opinion Research Center), University of Chicago
Institute for Social Research, University of Michigan
Survey Research Center, Temple University

In addition, most of the major graduate centers in the social sciences have one or more research centers in the social sciences
that participate in evaluation research activities.

III. MAJOR SOURCES OF EVALUATION FUNDING ON THE NATIONAL LEVEL

Evaluations are typically funded by sponsors who have oversight
responsibilities for the programs in question. On the national
level this ordinarily means that federal departments and agencies
are the sources of funds. Often Congress incorporates mandated
evaluations into authorizing legislation, sometimes directing an
agency to undertake an evaluation of a specific sort. National
evaluations are typically funded by contract let to one of the
major producers listed above.

The major federal agencies that frequently fund evaluations
are as follows:

Department of Education. Although its research budget was deci-
mated during the Reagan administration, this department still
conducts some of the major national evaluations. Currently it is
planning for a national impact assessment of its vocational
rehabilitation program. Tends to favor educational researchers as
evaluators.

Department of Labor. Strong funder of evaluations concerned
with its major man-power training, employment security (unemployment insurance, job placement), and so on. Tends to favor
economists.

Department of Agriculture. Funds evaluations in the fields of
nutrition, food stamps, and school lunch programs.

Department of Health and Human Resources. This extremely
large agency funds evaluations mainly through its component
divisions, among which the more prominent are the following:

Public Health Service (includes National Institutes of Health, Center for Disease Control), Social Security Administration, Health Care Finance Administration, Federal Drug Administration, and so on.

Department of Housing and Urban Development. Although also in eclipse during the Reagan regime, HUD has financed major social experiments and evaluations of many of its major programs.

Environmental Protection Agency. Currently concerned with the evaluation of its mass educational programs designed to raise public consciousness concerning hazardous substances.

Department of Defense. Runs major evaluations of human resources programs. Currently being forced by Congress into evaluations of its weapons systems.

General Accounting Office. Although it does not contract out its work, this agency has established an evaluation unit that undertakes evaluations at the request of Congress. The Division of Program Evaluation and Methodology now has about 50 PhD-level social scientists.

National Institute of Justice. A unit of the Department of Justice that has funded several field experiments on prospective criminal justice policies.

IV. SOME MAJOR EVALUATION RESEARCH AND EXEMPLARY PUBLISHED MONOGRAPHS IN EVALUATION

Each of the books cited above as general reference books contain extensive bibliographies of evaluation studies. Many of the references are to so-called fugitive documents (i.e., those not distributed by major publishers or published in easily accessible scholarly journals) and hence are difficult to locate in conventional university libraries. Some of the better ones that have been published in accessible form are listed below.

If you become stricken by a passion for evaluation, we suggest that you begin early to build your own library of fugitive documents. Many such documents, especially relating to studies that have been financed by federal agencies, are available in microfilm-xeroxed form through NTIS (National Technical Information Service) or ERIC (a computerized reference service supported by the Department of Education). *Evaluation News* (see journals above) contains a section on ongoing evaluation projects and recently issued reports.

A good university social science reference librarian can be of immense help in locating studies and arranging for access. Although most evaluation research or comments on evaluations are never published by commercial or university presses, some of the best ones and some of those that are concerned with major evaluation studies do get published. Listed below are some of the ones that we think are either excellent and/or concern major programs.

Berk, R. A. et al. 1981. *Water Shortage: Lessons in Conservation from the Great California Drought, 1967–1977.* Abt Books.
An analysis of the impact of water conservation programs in California.

Bradbury, K. L. and A. Downs, eds. 1981. *Do Housing Allowances Work?* Brookings Institution.
Collection of essays evaluating the Housing Allowance Experiments conducted by Abt Associates and the Rand Corporation.

Bunker, J. P., B. A. Barnes, and F. Mosteller. 1977. *Costs, Risks and Benefits of Surgery.* Oxford University Press.
A review of research on the relative effectiveness of surgical versus noninvasive procedures where there is a choice.

Cicirelli, V. G. et al. 1969. *The Impact of Head Start.* Athens. Westinghouse Learning Corporation and Ohio University.
A very controversial first evaluation of one of the more prominent social programs for preschool children.

Coleman, J. S. et al. 1966. *Equality of Educational Opportunity.* Washington, DC: Government Printing Office.
Needs assessment research that radically changed the direction of educational research.

Coleman, J. S. et al. 1982. *High School Achievement: Public, Catholic and Private Schools Compared.* Basic Books.
A controversial attempt to assess the differential effectiveness of high schools, purportedly finding that Catholic high school students achieve higher levels of math and verbal competence.

Cook. T. 1975. *Sesame Street Revisited.* Russell Sage.
Classic critique of evaluation of the children's educational TV program.

Cutright, P. and F. S. Jaffe. 1979. *Impact of Family Planning Programs on Fertility: The U.S. Experience.* Praeger.
A brilliant use of demographic data and survey data to estimate the impact of family planning clinics in the United States.

Davidson et al. 1981. *Evaluation Strategies in Criminal Justice.* Pergamon.
An account of the failure of an evaluation of juvenile justice programs in Michigan and a frank account of the sources of that failure.

Fairweather, G. W. and L. G. Tornatzky. 1977. *Experimental Methods for Social Policy Research.* Pergamon.
One of the best examples of the use of sophisticated evaluation research to design and refine a program for the successful reintegration into noninstitutional life of persons discharged from mental hospitals.

Friedman, D. and D. H. Weinberg. 1982. *The Economics of Housing Vouchers.* Academic Press.
Collection of papers on the Housing Allowance Experiments.

Gleser, G. C. et al. 1981. *Prolonged Psychosocial Effects of Disaster: A Study of Buffalo Creek.* Academic Press.
An attempt by a group of social scientists to estimate the residual psychological effects of the Buffalo Creek disaster in which a dam burst and wiped out a small West Virginia community. Extremely skillful.

Graham, John D., ed. 1988. *Preventing Automobile Injury: New Findings from Evaluation Research.* Auburn House.
Series of reports on impact of seat belt, drinking, and speed limit programs on automobile accident rates.

Gramlich, E. M. and P. P. Koshel. 1975. *Educational Performance Contracting: An Evaluation of an Experiment.* Brookings Institution.
A reanalysis of a pilot test of a program to contract out the teaching of certain subjects in high schools.

Kassebaum, G. et al. 1971. *Prison Treatment and Parole Survival.* John Wiley.
Classic controlled experiment evaluating the effectiveness of a group therapy program in California prisons.

Kelling, G. T. et al. 1974. *The Kansas City Patrol Experiment.* The Police Foundation.
Controlled field experiment on police patrolling strategies.

Kershaw, D. and J. Fair. 1976. *The New Jersey-Pennsylvania Income Maintenance Experiment.* Academic Press.
Narrative account of the first large-scale income maintenance field controlled experiment.

McLaughlin, M. 1975. *Evaluation and Reform: The Elementary and Secondary Education Act of 1965.* Ballinger.
An account of the failure of attempts to evaluate the effectiveness of the impact of this federal legislation on the education of disadvantaged children.

Mielke, K. W. and J. W. Swinehart. 1977. *Evaluation of the Feeling Good Television Series.* Children's Television Workshop.
A famous evaluation of an educational television program that led to the program being canceled.

Milavsky, J. R., R. C. Kessler, H. H. Stipp, and W. S. Rubin. 1982. *Television and Aggression: A Panel Study.* Academic Press.
An extremely skillful attempt to estimate the effects of watching violence on TV on the aggressive behavior of young schoolchildren.

Nathan, R. P. et al. 1983. *The Consequences of Cuts.* Princeton Urban and Regional Research Center.
A qualitative attempt to assess the Reagan regime's effects on local urban programs.

Peirce, W. S. 1981. *Bureaucratic Failure and Public Expenditure.* Academic Press.
A review of the effectiveness of public programs of all sorts and the development of a theory for explaining why they fail.

Pressman, J. L. and A. B. Wildavsky. 1973. *Implementation.* University of California Press.
A description of how an important program was implemented improperly.

Raizen, S. A. and P. H. Rossi, eds. 1981. *Program Evaluation in Education: When? How? To What Ends?* National Academy Press.
The report of a National Academy of Science Committee that reviewed the evaluation program of the Department of Education.

Robins, P. K. et al., eds. 1980. *A Guaranteed Annual Income: Evidence from a Social Experiment.* Academic Press.
Reports on the income maintenance experiments conducted in Seattle and Denver. Probably the best of the randomized field experiments of the 1970s.

Rossi, P. H., R. A. Berk, and K. Lenihan. 1980. *Money, Work and Crime: Experimental Evidence.* Academic Press.
Report of a large-scale randomized field experiment with persons released from the prisons of Texas and Georgia, the treatment being eligibility for unemployment compensation payments.

Rossi, P. H. and K. Lyall. 1975. *Reforming Social Welfare.* Russell Sage.
An assessment of the New Jersey-Pennsylvania Income Maintenance Experiment.

Rossi, P. H., J. D. Wright, E. Weber-Burdin, and J. Pereira. 1983. *Victims of the Environment: Losses from Natural Hazards in the United States: 1970–1980.* Plenum.

A "needs assessment" of the losses suffered by households in the United States over a decade, outlining the problems that are not affected by U.S. natural hazards policies of relief.

Smith, M. L., G. V. Glass, and T. I. Miller. 1980. *The Benefits of Psychotherapy: An Evaluation.* Johns Hopkins University Press.
A meta-evaluation that summarizes and puts together several hundred evaluations of the effectiveness of psychotherapy.

Struyk, R. J. and M. Bendick, eds. 1981. *Housing Vouchers for the Poor.* Urban Institute.
Another set of articles summarizing the findings of the Housing Allowance Experiments run by Abt and Rand.

Vanecko, J. J. and B. Jacobs. 1970. *Reports from the 100-City Cap Evaluation: The Impact of the Community Action Program on Institutional Change.* National Opinion Research Center.
A description of the local community action programs financed by the federal government in the 1960s.

Williams, W. 1980. *Government by Agency: Lessons from the Social Program Grants in Aid Experience.* Academic Press.
A qualitative assessment of the impact of block grants on local programs.

Wilner, D. M., R. P. Walkely, T. C. Pinkerton, and M. Tayback. 1962. *The Housing Environment and Family Life.* Johns Hopkins University Press.
A classic evaluation of the effects of public housing on households.

Wright, J. D. et al. 1979. *After the Clean-Up: The Long Range Effects of Natural Disasters.* Sage.
An evaluation of the long-range effects of natural hazard events (floods, hurricanes, and tornadoes) on growth trends in local communities.

References

Abt Associates. 1979. *Child Care Food Program*. Cambridge, MA: Author.

Baldus, D. C. and J.W.L. Cole. 1977. "Quantitative Proof of Intentional Discrimination." *Evaluation Quarterly* 1(1):53–86.

Barnett, V. 1982. *Comparative Statistical Inference*. New York: John Wiley.

Becker, H. S. 1958. "Problems of Inference and Proof in Participant Studies." *American Sociological Review* 23(6):652–60.

Berk, R. A. 1988a. "Causal Inference for Sociological Data." In *Handbook of Sociology*, edited by N. Smelser. Beverly Hills, CA: Sage.

——. 1988b. "The Role of Subjectivity in Criminal Justice Classification and Prediction Methods." *Criminal Justice Ethics* 6(1):183–200.

Berk, R. A., R. Boruch, D. Chambers, P. Rossi, and A. Witte. 1985. "Social Policy Experimentation: A Position Paper." *Evaluation Review* 9(4):387–429.

Berk, R. A. and M. Brewer. 1978. "Feet of Clay in Hobnailed Boots: An Assessment of Statistical Inference in Applied Research." Pp. 90–214 in *Evaluation Studies Review Annual*. Vol. 3, edited by T. D. Cook. Beverly Hills, CA: Sage.

Berk, R. A. and T. F. Cooley. 1987. "Errors in Forecasting Social Phenomena." *Climatic Change* 11(2):247–65.

Berk, R. A., T. F. Cooley, C. J. LaCivita, and K. Sredl. 1981. *Water Shortage: Lessons in Water Conservation Learned from the Great California Drought*. Cambridge, MA: Abt Books.

Berk, R. A. and A. Hartman. 1972. "Race and Class Differences in per Pupil Staffing Expenditures in Chicago Elementary Schools." *Integrated Education* 10(1):52–57.

Berk, R. A. and D. Rauma. 1983. "Capitalizing on Nonrandom Assignment to Treatments: A Regression Discontinuity Evaluation of a Crime Control Program." *Journal of the American Statistical Association* 78:21–28.

Berk, R. A. and P. H. Rossi. 1976. "Doing Good or Worse: Evaluation Research Politically Reexamined." *Social Problems* 23(4):337–49.

Berk, R. A. and L. W. Sherman. 1988. "Police Responses to Family Violence Incidents: An Analysis of an Experimental Design with Incomplete Randomization." *Journal of the American Statistical* Association 83:70–76.

Campbell, D. T. and A. Erlebacher. 1970. "How Regression Artifacts in Quasi-Experimental Evaluations Make Compensatory Education Look Harmful." Pp. 185–210 in *Compensatory Education: A National Debate*, edited by J. Hellmuth. New York: Brunner/Mazel.

119

Carson, R. 1955. *The Silent Spring*. New York: Bantam.

Chen, H. and P. H. Rossi. 1980. "The Multi-Goal, Theory-Driven Approach to Evaluation: A Model Linking Basic and Applied Social Science." *Social Forces* 59(1):106–22.

Cicirelli, V. G. et al. 1969. *The Impact of Head Start*. Athens: Westinghouse Learning Corporation and Ohio State University.

Coleman, J. et al. 1967. *Equality of Educational Opportunity*. Washington, DC: Government Printing Office.

Conant, James B. 1959. *The American High School Today*. New York: McGraw-Hill.

Cook, T. and D. Campbell. 1979. *Quasi-Experimentation*. Chicago: Rand McNally.

Cook, T. et al. 1975. *Sesame Street Revisited*. New York: Russell Sage.

Cronbach, L. J. 1975. "Five Decades of Controversy over Mental Testing." *American Psychologist* 30(1):1–14.

———. 1982. *Designing Evaluations of Educational and Social Programs*. Menlo Park, CA: Jossey-Bass.

Cronbach, L. J. and Associates. 1980. *Towards Reform of Program Evaluation*. Menlo Park, CA: Jossey-Bass.

Deutscher, I. 1977. "Toward Avoiding the Goal Trap in Evaluation Research." Pp. 221–38 in *Readings in Evaluation Research*, edited by F. Caro. New York: Russell Sage.

Edgington, E. S. 1987. *Randomization Tests*. 2nd ed. New York: Marcel Dekker.

Ericksen, E. P. and J. B. Kadane. 1985. "Estimating the Population in a Census Year: 1980 and Beyond." *Journal of the American Statistical Association* 80:98–131.

Fairweather, George and Louis G. Tornatzky. 1977. *Experimental Methods for Social Policy Research*. New York: Pergamon.

Franke, R. H. 1979. "The Hawthorne Experiments: Review." *American Sociological Review* 44(5):861–67.

Franke, R. H. and J. D. Kaul. 1978. "The Hawthorne Experiments: First Statistical Interpretation." *American Sociological Review* 43(5):623–43.

Freedman, D. A. and H. Zeisel. 1988. "Cancer and Risk Assessment: From Mouse to Man." *Statistical Science* 3:1–27.

Geisel, M. S., R. Roll, and R. S. Wettick, Jr. 1969. "The Effectiveness of State and Local Regulation of Handguns: A Statistical Analysis." *Duke Law Journal* (August):647–76.

General Accounting Office. 1986. *Teenage Pregnancy: 500,000 Births a Year But Few Tested Programs*. Washington, DC: Author.

Goodman, S. N. and R. Royall. 1988. "Evidence and Scientific Research." *American Journal of Public Health* 78(12):1568–75.

Gramlich, E. M. and P. Koshel. 1975. *Educational Performance Contracting*. Washington: Brookings Institution.

Guba, E. and Y. Lincoln. 1981. *Effective Evaluation*. Menlo Park, CA: Jossey-Bass.

Guttentag, M. and E. Struening, eds. 1975. *Handbook of Evaluation Research*. 2 vols. Beverly Hills, CA: Sage.

Harrington, Michael. 1962. *The Other America.* New York: Macmillan.

Hausman, J. A. and D. A. Wise. 1985. *Social Experimentation.* Chicago: University of Chicago Press.

Heckman, J. and R. Robb. 1985. "Alternative Methods for Evaluating the Impact of Interventions." In *Longitudinal Analysis of Labor Market Data,* edited by J. J. Heckman and B. Singer. New York: Cambridge University Press.

Heilman, J. G. 1980. "Paradigmatic Choices in Evaluation Methodology." *Evaluation Review* 4(5): 693–712.

Holland, P. W. 1986. "Statistics and Causal Inference." *Journal of the American Statistical Association* 81:945–60.

Holland, P. W. and D. B. Rubin. 1988. "Causal Inference in Retrospective Studies." *Evaluation Review* 12(3):203–31.

Kazdin, A. E. 1982. *Single Case Research Designs.* New York: Oxford University Press.

Kershaw, D. and J. Fair. 1976. *The New Jersey Income Maintenance Experiment.* New York: Academic Press.

Kish, L. 1965. *Survey Sampling.* New York: John Wiley.

Kmenta, J. 1971. *Elements of Econometrics.* New York: Macmillan.

Krug, A. S. 1967. "The Relationship Between Firearm Licensing Laws and Crime Rates." *Congressional Record,* 113, part 15 (July 25): 200060–64.

Lenihan, K. 1976. *Opening the Second Gate.* Washington, DC: Government Printing Office.

Lewis, D. A., T. Pavkov, H. Rosenberg, S. Reed, A. Lurigio, Z. Kalifon, B. Johnson, and S. Riger. 1987. *State Hospitalization Utilization in Chicago.* Evanston, IL: Center for Urban Affairs and Policy Research.

Lewis, Oscar. 1965. *La Vida.* New York: Random House.

Liebow, Elliot. 1967. *Tally's Corner.* Boston: Little, Brown.

Lord, F. M. 1980. *Applications of Item Response Theory to Practical Testing Problems.* Hillsdale, NJ: Lawrence Erlbaum.

Mathematica Policy Research. 1980. *Job Corps Evaluated.* Princeton, NJ: Mathematica.

Maynard, R. A. and R. J. Murnane. 1979. "The Effects of the Negative Income Tax on School Performance." *Journal of Human Resources* 14(4):463–76.

Mensh, I. N. and J. Henry. 1953. "Direct Observation and Psychological Tests in Anthropological Field Work." *American Anthropology* 55(4):461–80.

Milavsky, J. R., H. H. Stipp, R. C. Kessler, and W. S. Rubens. 1982. *Television and Aggression: A Panel Study.* New York: Academic Press.

Murray, Sandra A. 1980. *The National Evaluation of the PUSH for Excellence Project* (manuscript). Washington: American Institutes for Research.

Murray, William A. 1981. *Final Report: Evaluation of Cities in School Program* (manuscript). Washington, DC: American Institutes for Research.

Nathan, R.F.C. Doolittle and Associates. 1983. *The Consequences of Cuts.* Princeton, NJ: Princeton Urban and Regional Research Center.

Pollard, W. E. 1986. *Bayesian Statistics for Evaluation Research.* Beverly Hills, CA: Sage.

Pratt, J. W. and R. Schlaifer. 1984. "On the Nature and Discovery of Structure." *Journal of the American Statistical Association* 79(1):9–21.

Raizen, S. and P. H. Rossi. 1981. *Program Evaluation in Education: When? How? To What Ends?* Washington, DC: National Academy Press.

Reiss, Albert E. 1971. *The Police and the Public.* New Haven, CT: Yale University Press.

Riis, Jacob A. 1890. *How the Other Half Lives.* New York: Scribner.

Robertson, L. S. 1980. "Crash Involvement of Teenaged Drivers when Driver Education Is Eliminated from High School." *American Journal of Public Health* 70(6):599–603.

Robins, P. K. et al. 1980. *A Guaranteed Annual Income: Evidence from a Social Experiment.* New York: Academic Press.

Rosenbaum, Paul R. and Donald B. Rubin. 1985. "The Bias Due to Incomplete Matching." *Biometrics* 41:103–16.

Rossi, P. H. 1978. "Issues in the Evaluation of Human Services Delivery." *Evaluation Quarterly* 2(4):573–99.

———. 1987. "The Iron Law of Evaluation and Other Metallic Rules." Pp. 3–20 in *Research in Social Problems and Public Policy.* Vol. 4, edited by J. Miller and M. Lewis. Greenwich, CT: JAI.

Rossi, P. H., Richard A. Berk, and Bettye K. Eidson. 1974. *The Roots of Urban Discontent.* New York: John Wiley.

Rossi, P. H., R. Berk, and K. Lenihan. 1980. *Money, Work and Crime.* New York: Academic Press.

Rossi, P. H. and B. Biddle. 1966. *The New Media and Education.* Chicago: Aldine.

Rossi, P. H. and Robert Dentler. 1961. *The Politics of Urban Renewal: The Chicago Findings.* New York: Free Press.

Rossi, P. H., G. Fisher, and G. Willis. 1986. *The Condition of the Homeless of Chicago.* Amherst, MA, and Chicago: Social and Demographic Research Institute, University of Massachusetts, and NORC (A Social Science Research Institute, University of Chicago).

Rossi, P. H. and H. Freeman. 1989. *Evaluation: A Systematic Approach.* 4th ed. Beverly Hills, CA: Sage.

Rossi, P. H. and K. Lyall. 1974. *Reforming Public Welfare.* New York: Russell Sage.

Rossi, P. H., J. D. Wright, E. Weber-Burdin, and J. Pereira. 1983. *Victims of the Environment: Loss from Natural Hazards in the United States, 1970–1980.* New York: Academic Press.

Rubin, D. B. 1977. "Assignment of Treatment Group on the Basis of a Covariate." *Journal of Education Statistics* 2:1–26.

———. 1986. "Which Ifs Have Causal Answers." *Journal of the American Statistical Association* 81:961–62.

Scriven, M. 1972. "Pros and Cons About Goal-Free Evaluation." *Evaluation Comment* 3(1):1–4.

Seitz, S. T. 1972. "Firearms, Homicide and Gun Control Effectiveness." *Law and Society Review* 6(May):595–613.

Sherman, L. W. and E. G. Cohn. 1989. "The Impact of Research on Legal Policy: The Minneapolis Domestic Violence Experiment." *Law and Society Review* 23(1):117–45.

Sinclair, Upton. 1906. *The Jungle*. New York: Doubleday.

Smith, V. K., W. H. Desvousges, A. Fisher, and F. R. Johnson. 1987. *Communicating Radon Risk Effectively: A Mid-Course Evaluation* (Publication #EPA-230-07-87-029). Washington, DC: Environmental Protection Agency.

Steinbeck, John. 1939. *The Grapes of Wrath*. New York: Viking.

Struyk, R. J. and M. Bendick. 1981. *Housing Vouchers for the Poor: Lessons from a National Experiment*. Washington, DC: Urban Institute.

Suchman, E. 1967. *Evaluation Research*. New York: Russell Sage.

Sudman, S. 1976. *Applied Sampling*. New York: Academic Press.

Thompson, M. 1980. *Cost-Benefit Analysis*. Beverly Hills, CA: Sage.

Trochim, W.M.K. 1984. *Research Design for Program Evaluation: The Regression Discontinuity Approach*. Beverly Hills, CA: Sage.

U.S. Conference of Mayors. 1987. *The Continuing Growth of Hunger, Homelessness, and Poverty in U.S. Cities: 1987*. Washington, DC: Author.

Wardwell, W. L. 1979. "Comment on Kaul and Franke." *American Sociological Review* 44(5):858-61.

Weiss, C. 1972. *Evaluation Research*. Englewood Cliffs, NJ: Prentice-Hall.

Wholey, J. S. 1977. "Evaluability Assessment." Pp. 49-56 in *Evaluation Research Methods*, edited by L. Putnam. Beverly Hills, CA: Sage.

Wright, J. D., P. H. Rossi, and K. Daly. 1983. *Under the Gun: Weapons, Crime and Violence in America*. New York: Aldine.

Index

Abstract perfection, 9
Assignment, 27–28, 30, 35, 55, 73, 78–79, 81–94

Bias, 19, 25, 26, 85, 86–87, 92
Biased sample, 26–27

Causal effect, 19, 56, 81, 82
Causal inference, 19–21, 55, 73, 79, 80
Causal models, 35
Causality, 19–21, 40, 73
Chance, 17, 25–29, 54, 82
Comparison group, 16, 31, 73, 77–80, 85–87, 90–92
Confidence intervals, 27–29
Control variable, 19, 80
Control groups, 27, 35, 55, 79, 81, 82–84
Cost effectiveness, 16
Cost-benefit analysis, 8, 57–61, 70, 94–95
Coverage, 57, 64–66, 73, 87
Cross-sectional designs, 90–92

Data quality, 42
Demonstration programs, 53
Discounting, 58, 95
Double blind experiment, 96

Empirical generalizations, 8, 24
Errors in variables, 19
Ethnographic studies, 8, 26, 44–46, 56

Evaluability assessment, 15, 71–75
Evaluation contexts, 36, 50
Examination of existing policies and programs, 37, 63–97
Experimental groups, 27, 35, 55, 79, 81, 82–84

Fiscal accountability, 69–71
Forecasting, 46–47

Generalizability, 21–25

Impact assessment, 58, 71–76, 79
Implementation, 30, 48, 51–53, 56
Implementation studies, 67–68, 98
In-house evaluation, 14
Inferential errors, 20
Interaction effects, 96
Interrupted time series, 87–89

Latent variable, 19, 80

Marginal effectiveness, 15–16, 54
Matching, 80, 91, 96
Measurement, 17–19, 30, 44
Measurement error
  systematic, 18
  random, 19
Monitoring, 8, 40, 51, 54, 75, 98

Needs assessment, 41–47, 49, 64–67

Opportunity costs, 70
Outcome, 18, 30, 59
Outcome variable, 19, 26, 72, 92

Panel designs, *see* Pooled cross-sectional and time series designs
Pilot studies, 44, 50–52
Placebo, 96
Policy and program formulation, 36, 37–62
Policy environment, 12, 15
Policy space, 12–13, 30, 37, 59
Pooled cross-sectional and time series designs, 92–94
Practical perfection, 9
Probability samples, 27
Problem driven research, 47–49
Program effectiveness, 15–16, 54–59, 70, 72–80
Program integrity research, 66–69

Random sampling, 24, 28
Randomized experiments, 8, 52, 55–56, 82–84
Regression discontinuity, 85–87, 89, 92
Relative effectiveness, 16, 30, 54, 56
Relevance, 30
Reliability, 19
Replication, 24
Research design, 9, 29–30, 80–94

Sampling error, 26
Selection bias, 26

Selection model, 92
Settings, 22, 47, 77
Single blind experiment, 96
Stakeholders, 13–15, 42
Statistical controls, 79–80, 89, 91–92
Statistical inference, 25, 27, 29, 83, 84
Stochastic, 81
Structural equations, 95–96
Successful evaluation, 9–10
Surveys, 8

Target population, 8, 21, 64
Treatment, 19, 23, 27, 28, 30, 50, 55, 57, 68, 70, 82–94
Typology of research design, 81

Unbiased sample, 24, 26
Underadjustment, 19

Validity, 16–17
  construct validity, 17–19, 25–29
  external validity, 17, 21–25
  internal validity, 17, 19–21, 54, 82, 92, 94
  statistical conclusion validity, 17, 25, 54

the "YOAA problem," 52–54

About the Authors

RICHARD A. BERK is Professor in the Department of Sociology and Program in Social Statistics at UCLA. He is vice chair of the Board of Directors of the Social Science Research Council (SSRC), a fellow of the American Association for the Advancement of Science, former chair of the Methodology Section of the American Sociological Association, and a former visiting scholar at the GAO. He currently serves on a National Academy of Science Committee on the social consequences of AIDS and an SSRC Committee on the human dimensions of global environmental change. Professor Berk has published a large number of books and articles many of which are evaluations or are about evaluation research. Three recent evaluation studies focus respectively on the impact of different police interventions in incidents of wife battery, a training program for judges handling family violence cases, and the impact of an AIDS-education prevention program for college students. His most recent book is *The Social Consequences of AIDS in the United States* (1989). He serves with Harvard Freeman as editor of the *Evaluation Review*.

PETER H. ROSSI is currently S. A. Rice Professor of Sociology and Acting Director, Social and Demographic Research Institute, at the University of Massachusetts at Amherst. He has been on the faculties of Harvard University, the University of Chicago, and Johns Hopkins University. He was Director, from 1960 to 1967, of the National Opinion Research Center at the University of Chicago. He has been a consultant on social research methods and evaluation to (among others) the National Science Foundation, the National Institute of Mental Health, the General Accounting Office, and the Rockefeller Foundation. His research has largely been concerned with the application of social research methods to social issues and he is currently engaged in research on homelessness and extreme poverty. His recent books include *Without Shelter* (1989), *Down and Out in America* (1989), *Of Human Bonding: Parent-Child Relations Throughout the Life Course* (1990, with Alice S. Rossi), and *Handbook of Survey Research* (1983, edited, with J. D. Wright and A. B. Anderson). He is past-president of the American Sociological Association and was the 1985 recipient of Common Wealth Award for contributions to sociology. He has received awards from the Evaluation Research Society, the Eastern Evaluation Society, and the Policy Studies Association for contributions to evaluation research. He has served as editor of the *American Journal of Sociology* and *Social Science Research*. He has been elected a Fellow of the American Academy of Arts and Sciences and the American Association for the Advancement of Science.